LLEWELLYN'S
Little Book of
WITCHCRAFT

Photo by Bobbie Hodges

Deborah Blake is the author of over a dozen books on modern Witchcraft, including *The Little Book of Cat Magic* and *Everyday Witchcraft*, as well as the acclaimed *Everyday Witch Tarot* and *Everyday Witch Oracle* decks. She has also written three paranormal romance and urban fantasy series for Berkley, and her new cozy mystery series launches with *Furbidden Fatality* in 2021. Deborah lives in a 130-year-old farmhouse in upstate New York with numerous cats who supervise all her activities, both magical and mundane. She can be found at: DeborahBlakeAuthor.com

LLEWELLYN'S
Little Book of
WITCHCRAFT

DEBORAH BLAKE

LLEWELLYN PUBLICATIONS
WOODBURY, MINNESOTA

FIRST EDITION
First Printing, 2023

Cover cartouche by Freepik
Cover design by Shira Atakpu
Interior art by Llewellyn Art Department

Llewellyn Publications is a registered trademark of Llewellyn Worldwide Ltd.

Library of Congress Cataloging-in-Publication Data Pending
ISBN: 978-0-7387-7481-7

Llewellyn Worldwide Ltd. does not participate in, endorse, or have any authority or responsibility concerning private business transactions between our authors and the public.

All mail addressed to the author is forwarded, but the publisher cannot, unless specifically instructed by the author, give out an address or phone number.

Any internet references contained in this work are current at publication time, but the publisher cannot guarantee that a specific location will continue to be maintained. Please refer to the publisher's website for links to authors' websites and other sources.

Llewellyn Publications
A Division of Llewellyn Worldwide Ltd.
2143 Wooddale Drive
Woodbury, MN 55125-2989
www.llewellyn.com

Printed in China

Dedicated to all my wonderful readers.

You make the magic happen.

Contents

(

Activities

Spells

Tips

INTRODUCTION

Growing up, I was always the "weird one" in the family. If anyone was going to do something in an odd or unusual fashion or act completely different from everyone else, it was going to be me. Needless to say, it didn't make me terribly popular growing up, although thankfully my family didn't have a problem with it.

I was usually a little out of step with the rest of the world. I read constantly and widely, preferred the company of trees to people, liked to grow vegetables and herbs, and of course, adored cats. I loved fairy tales and stories of magic and fantasy, and I had the uncomfortable ability of sensing what other people were feeling or thinking. For most of my earlier years, I just assumed this was who I was—the weird girl who didn't fit in.

If any of this sounds at all familiar to you, you may see where this is going. As I got older, I found friends who liked me for who I was—and that was great—but there was always something missing. Some part of the story that didn't add up.

Growing up Jewish, I was proud of my heritage but the religion, with its stern father figure God and strong patriarchal tone, never resonated with me. I eventually spent some time with the Unitarians (nice but still too Christian for me), and studying Buddhism (closer but still not quite what I was looking for). I finally reached a point in my thirties where I figured I was agnostic and open-minded, and left it at that.

 Until the night a friend finally convinced me to come to her house on Halloween, which she called Samhain, for a celebration and ritual. She'd been asking for some time, and I kept saying no because I wasn't sure I would be com-

fortable with a bunch of people I didn't know and the rituals she put on. But for some reason, that time I said yes.

There were way too many people there, and many of them were a bit odd, even for me. They kept hugging me and saying things like, "Merry Meet"; I had no idea what the heck was going on, but the feast was delicious and everyone was friendly.

Eventually we went outside to the park next to my friend's house and gathered in a circle. It was dark out, and quiet, except for the crackling of the bonfire and maybe a little drumming. The scent of sage filled the air. The woman who was acting as high priestess that night formally cast the circle, calling the quarters as we all turned and pointed in that direction—east, south, west, and finally north. Then she invoked the God and Goddess and asked them to join us in our sacred ritual space. And my entire life changed.

For all those years, I had reached out into the universe, over and over, and felt nothing. On that crisp and chilly October eve, someone reached back. I could feel Goddess and God as clearly as if they were standing in front of me. They were, I think, both welcoming and quietly amused by my surprise and said, "Well, it took you long enough." I was home.

It wasn't so much that I became a witch on that night. More, it was that I discovered there was a name for what and who I had been all along. In fact, when I told a mutual friend (also a Witch) about my experience and said with some wonder, "It turns out I'm a witch!" she simply laughed and said, "Oh, I know. I've known for ages." When I asked her why she hadn't told me, she explained that I needed to come to it in my own time. I guess I was finally ready.

These days, there are as many different ways to practice Witchcraft (capitalized when referring to the formal religion) as there are witches. Some folks call themselves Wiccans, some witches, and some simply Pagans. Others may use the terms interchangeably, although not all witches are Wiccans, nor all Pagans witches.

Modern witches usually (but not always) follow a nature-based religion that is polytheistic—based on the worship of multiplies deity—including both Goddess and God—and celebrating both the cycles of the moon (esbats) and the path of the sun throughout the year (sabbats). Some people prefer to call what they do a spiritual path rather than an organized religion. Most witches believe in magic and use it as a part of their practice.

Today's Witchcraft has strong roots in the past, whether you believe there was a direct line from the witchcraft practitioners of old or that we have much in common with earlier Pagans who lived on and appreciated the land; worshipped a goddess alongside a god; and practiced the crafts of healing, herbalism, and magic. Each witch must find their own path, the one that feeds their spirit and fills their heart, and then continue to learn and grow as they walk that path to the form of Witchcraft that works best for them. Hopefully this book will help with that journey.

Maybe you have been practicing Witchcraft for years or are finally ready to discover the name for who you have been all along. Or perhaps you need something to hand to a friend who is still trying to find their path. This book is designed to be fun and useful no matter what point in your Witchcraft journey you are at, beginner or more experienced practitioner.

In these pages you'll find spells, activities, tips, as well as a basic history of Witchcraft and a brief guide to common practices. There is no one way to use the book— you can start at the beginning and go straight through to the end or hop around if that suits your needs better. There are also suggestions for additional reading at the end in case you want to delve further into the wonderful, magical world of Witchcraft.

No matter how you use it, I hope you have fun, learn a little something, and that it helps you just a little as you walk the journey that is specifically yours.

Merry meet.

Chapter One
COMMONLY USED TERMS

There are a few common terms used in Witchcraft that the beginner may not be familiar with, so here is an easy reference section.

BANISHING: Banishing means to get rid of something. In magic, it can be physical (health issues, addiction), psychological (depression, bad habits, repeating patterns that don't work for you anymore), spiritual (dark energies, although it can be difficult to tell if such things are coming from the inside or the outside), or even people. Be very careful if you use magic to banish someone from your life—it is almost always permanent, and you may not get a chance to change your mind. When groups do banishing work together, it is usually of a more general nature. For instance, everyone may write down things they want to banish from their lives and take turns throwing them into a Samhain bonfire.

BLESSING: We often talk about blessing and consecrating new tools or a space being used for magical work. Essentially this is asking the Goddess and God to send their blessings. This adds a level of power and spirit to whatever or whoever (like a new baby) is being blessed.

CAKES AND ALE: The part of the ritual where some form of food and drink are passed around the circle, usually coming right before the end, after all the serious magical work is done. It serves to ground the participants back to the real world and is also symbolic of the bonds we share as witches.

"Ale" isn't necessarily something alcoholic—it could be juice, cider, or even water.

CHARGE OF THE GODDESS: A traditional Wiccan poem that is sometimes recited as part of ritual, usually at the beginning (but not always). It can be extremely powerful and moving.

CLEANSING AND CLEARING: In magical work, cleansing isn't about practical, physical cleaning but rather clearing the energy of people, places, things. You might cleanse the circle before you start a ritual, or a new tool, especially if it belonged to someone previously and you want to rid it of any leftover energy.

CONSECRATE: Consecrating is related to blessing but is more that you are pledging whatever is being consecrated (a new tool, a charm bag, a tarot deck) to positive magical use.

DEDICATION: Dedication is the act of making a formal commitment, either to a coven or the gods. Some groups ask new members to do a dedication after a year and a day, others only want people to do it when

they feel ready, and some don't necessarily do dedications at all. witches can self-dedicate on their own as well.

DEITY: A general word for any god or goddess.

DEOSIL: Movement in a clockwise direction, sometimes for increase or positive work, or for closing a circle. Almost all movement within a magical circle is done is a deosil fashion.

DIVINATION: Divination is a way of looking for answers or for knowledge of the future. It can involve a number of different tools, including tarot cards, rune stones, oracle cards, scrying, and more. It comes from the Latin *divinare,* which means "to foresee, to foretell, to predict." It is actually related to the word "divine," which suggests that this knowledge may come from the gods.

ECLECTIC WITCH: An Eclectic Witch is one who takes elements of different Witchcraft approaches (and occasionally other spiritual paths) and combines them into a practice that works for them.

ELEMENT: This is a term generally applied to the four elements of earth, air, fire, and water. They are also referred to as elemental powers. Spirit is sometimes considered to be the fifth, most important element of all.

ESBAT: Esbat is the name for the lunar rituals and observances that take place at the full moon or the new moon.

FEASTS: Many sabbat rituals (and some full moons, depending on the individual witch or witches involved) are followed by feasts, usually a special meal in celebration of a particular holiday. A feast usually features food that ties in the season and the theme of the sabbat. Solitary Witches may not bother to make a special meal, although they certainly can. Covens and other groups almost always do, unless the sabbat is observed in some-place like a large park where there is no good way to serve a number of people.

HANDFASTING: A Pagan wedding rite. This may be a formal legal ceremony or a ritual that is spiritually but not legally binding. Some handfastings are done for a year and a day, and others are for life, as with any other wedding. The term comes from "hand-fastening," because the couple is often loosely bound together with a cord during the ceremony to symbolize that they are binding themselves together as one.

HIGH PRIEST/HIGH PRIESTESS: A Pagan spiritual leader, usually someone who has years of experience and practice before assuming the title. This is more of a Wiccan term than a general Witchcraft one, although it can vary from group to group.

INTENT: The purpose of a spell or magical working, also the focused energy used to bring it about. Intent is one of the most important components of spell work. In order to be successful, you need to be clear about your intentions when casting a spell.

INVOCATION: An invocation is a call, a prayer, or a summoning. When we talk about invocations in Witchcraft, it is usually associated with inviting the elements and/or the God/dess to come into our magical space.

LAW OF THREE: This is a generally accepted Wiccan precept that everything you put out into the universe comes back to you times three. So if you do positive magic, you will reap the rewards three times over, but if you do harmful magic, it will come back and bite you. Some people call this the Law of Returns, which is a bit simpler and basically means that what you put out is what you get back.

MAIDEN, MOTHER, AND CRONE:

These terms are associated with the three different stages of a woman's life, essentially before, during, and after a woman's ability to have a child, but not necessarily tied to exact physical timetables. In more traditional Wiccan forms of practice, they may be the names of roles in a group or ritual. It is also tied to the different stages of the lunar cycle, waxing, full, and waning.

MUNDANE: This isn't an insult in any way. It's the word some people use to indicate the part of their life that isn't magical. For example, I have my mundane friends and my witchy friends.

OLD GODS: Some witches use this term to refer to any pre-Christianity deities. You might say, "I worship the Old Gods" if someone asks what religious path you follow.

PAGAN: Someone who worships the Old Gods (almost always including at least one goddess) and follows a nature-based religion. Not all Pagans are witches, but all witches are Pagans. "Pagan" comes from the Latin *paganus*, a term that used to refer to a dweller in the countryside and references the fact that the rural folks of Europe were the last to be converted or absorbed by the then-new Christian religion. I refer to myself equally as a Pagan and a Witch, but there are definitely Pagans who are not witches and who would be insulted if you assumed they were.

PENTACLE: A commonly used Witchcraft symbol that consists of a five-pointed star with a circle around it. The five points represent the five elements—earth, air, fire, water, and Spirit—and the circle is the universe that holds them all, or unity. A pentagram, which is closely related to the pentacle, is a five-pointed star drawn in one continuous line. Witches use it, but it has also shown up in many other cultures and religions throughout history. A pentacle is often used for protection in addition to a symbol of Witchcraft.

QUARTER: We talk a lot about the four quarters. These are directions used in magical work, and each has its own set of associations: East–Air, South–Fire, West–Water, and North–Earth.

QUARTER CALLS: These are the invocations we say to invite the powers of the quarters to enter our sacred space. They may be as simple as, "Powers of east, the element of air, please join me in my circle," or considerably more elaborate. They should always be said with respect.

SABBAT: One of eight holidays in the Pagan calendar, which includes the two solstices, two equinoxes, and four quarter-cross holidays that fall at equal times between them. They are Imbolc (Feb 2), Ostara (spring equinox, around March 21), Beltane (May 1), midsummer (summer solstice, around June 21), Lammas (August 2), Mabon (autumn equinox, around September 21), Samhain (October 31), and Yule (winter solstice, around December 21). The dates of the solstices and equinoxes vary slightly every year.

SOLITARY: A witch who practices alone rather than with a group. Most witches who belong to a coven also do solitary work, but a Solitary Witch always or almost always practiced on their own.

SPEAKING STICK: A stick or some other object that is passed around the circle during a group ritual. Usually used at the end, it allows each participant to have a moment to speak what is in their heart without interruption.

WHEEL OF THE YEAR: The Pagan calendar of holidays and the turning of the seasons. Magical work is often done in accordance with where we are on the Wheel of the Year, since the energy of the earth changes with the seasons. So magic for new starts might be done at the spring equinox, while magic for letting go might be done at Samhain, the last of the three harvest festivals.

WICCA: A specific modern form of Witchcraft practice brought over from England in the 1960s by Raymond Buckland after it was started in the 1950s by Gerald Gardner. It has since splintered off into many different variations, none of which follow exactly the same beliefs or tenets. The original

Wicca practices involved initiation into at least three levels and ornate, formal rituals. All Wiccans are witches, but not all witches are Wiccans.

WICCAN REDE: The longer form is an elaborate poem written in archaic language by Gwen Thompson in the 1970s. The shorter version was popularized by Doreen Valiente, sometimes called the Mother of Modern Witchcraft. Often used in Wicca's early days during ritual, it spells out the rules of Wicca as they were when the practice began. The briefest form, "An it harm none, do as ye will," is often considered Wicca's "Golden Rule." It is followed by some witches (but not all), and basically means that you can do what you please as long as you aren't hurting anyone.

WIDDERSHINS: Movement done in a counterclockwise direction, usually used for banishing, unbinding, or for opening a magical circle at the end of a ritual.

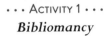

· · · ACTIVITY 1 · · ·
Bibliomancy

A simple form of divination, bibliomancy is a fast and easy way to get an answer to a basic question. In this case, you can just ask, "What do I need to know today?" or "What in this book is important to me?" and then flip open the book to a random page and see what's there.

Chapter Two

VARIATIONS ON A WITCHCRAFT THEME

As mentioned in the introduction, there are many ways to practice Witchcraft, and what works for one person might not work for another. Don't let anyone tell you that there is only one right way.

If you are just starting out, it might take some time and experimentation to figure out what kind of a Witchcraft practice fits your personal style, needs, and limitations. A busy parent of four with a full-time job won't necessarily take the same approach as someone who is retired and has plenty of time. If you aren't comfortable in social situations, you will want something very different than the person who enjoys large celebrations.

Not everyone sees deity in the same way or considers Witchcraft to be a religion/spiritual path rather than a skill, nor does everyone want to include spellcasting in their practice or be out of the broom closet (a term that means being open about being a Witch).

When beginning witches ask me where to start, I usually suggest two things: read widely (there is a suggested reading list at the end of this book), and just try things to see what feels right. Listen to your heart and that little inner voice we all have and you will figure it out, I promise.

Here are some of the various approaches you can look at, although the possibilities are endless. You can combine any or all of these as you desire. Keep in mind that there is no need to label yourself in any way if you don't want to.

SOLITARY

Solitary is the term used for witches who practice on their own. This may be out of choice, preference, or necessity because they can't find others to share their path. (In rural or conservative areas of the country, it can be hard to connect with other Pagans.) Almost all witches do at least some solitary work, even if they are also part of a coven. For instance, my coven only meets on the eight sabbats these days, so I do magical work on my own in between. And of course, my Witchcraft beliefs shape how I live my life every day.

COVEN

While some witches prefer to practice on their own, others enjoy sharing the Craft with like-minded folks. I am a fairly solitary person in most other facets of my life, so it was a little surprising to discover I was a group witch. You just never know. Not everyone who gathers in a group uses the term "coven." Some people call it a "circle" (my group is called Blue Moon Circle because not all of us were comfortable with "coven"), "group," or something else depending on the particular traditions they might follow.

Covens can work in a number of different ways. Traditional Wiccan covens were led by a high priest and a high priestess, and a new member had to go through three levels of initiation. The one I started out in was an offshoot of a traditional Wiccan group but had no levels and only a high priestess. These days, many covens tend to be eclectic and casual, although there are still plenty of more formal traditions to choose from if that is the style you prefer.

If you can't find a group that suits you, you can always consider starting your own. Don't worry about not having enough people—Blue Moon Circle was just me and two others to begin with, and I have a friend who has been practicing with one other person for many years.

It can be difficult to find a coven in some places in the country, especially if you live in a more rural or conservative area. If there is a Unitarian Church in your area, check to see if they have a local chapter of CUUPS (Covenant of Unitarian Universalist Pagans). Keep an eye on the sign boards at places like health food stores or New Age stores, if you are lucky enough to have one. Alternately, if you can find even one or two other like-minded people, you can start your own. Before you get started just make sure that you are all looking for the same thing to avoid conflicts later.

In addition to these basic different approaches, there are also many variations on a Witchcraft path. Some people focus on just one, and others, like me, tend to combine aspects of a number of options. Keep in mind that this is just the tip of the iceberg; if you go looking, you will find many additional possibilities.

CELTIC WITCH

This is actually a broad term that covers those who practice Witchcraft based on Celtic deities and mythology.

There are also witches who focus on other cultures, such as Egyptian, Italian (Stregha is a particular form of Italian Witchcraft made popular in this country primarily by Raven Grimassi), Norse, and so on.

CEREMONIAL WITCH

Ceremonial Witchcraft, also sometimes called "High Magic" involves detailed and complicated rituals and is much more formal than many other types. It may include older occult teachings such as the Kabbalah.

DIANIC WITCH

Named after the goddess Diana, Dianic Witchcraft focuses on the worship of a goddess or goddesses (not a god). It is based on the feminine experience and empowering women. In recent years, there has been argument about whether or not this would include trans women, causing some tension in the greater Witchcraft community.

ECLECTIC WITCH

An Eclectic Witch is someone who takes bits and pieces of whichever types of magical and spiritual practices work for them and combines them. I consider myself to be an Eclectic Witch, although many of my practices are Wiccan in origin, because that was how I was taught.

GARDNERIAN WITCH

Someone who follows the original teachings of Gerald Gardner. Wiccan, coven-based, and usually very secretive.

GREEN WITCH

The Green Witch is someone who works with herbs and often other plants as well. The term "Garden Witch" is sometimes used for those who grow their own. Green Witches have a strong connection to nature, often feeling more at home with plants than people, and most of their magical work makes use of herbs, trees, and other growing things. I have a very large garden and grow many of the herbs I use in my magic, so this is definitely an aspect of my identity as a Witch, although not the whole of it.

HEARTH WITCH

This is Witchcraft that centers around the home and can integrate Kitchen Witchery as well.

HEREDITARY WITCH

Hereditary Witchcraft is handed down through a family, from one generation to another and is generally not shared with outsiders.

KITCHEN WITCH

Kitchen Witches, as the name implies, tend to focus their magical endeavors through cooking, baking, and other culinary creations. This might mean creating healing teas or adding ingredients with magical associations for prosperity to a stew or soup. Cooking is often done from the heart, after all. Kitchen Witches add focus and intent to regular kitchen prep to take what they do from mundane to magical. Obviously, one can be both a Green Witch and a Kitchen Witch, since it makes sense to grow some of your own ingredients, even if that means only a few herbs on a sunny windowsill.

TRADITIONAL WITCH

These are witches who follow what they consider to be a traditional Witchcraft path, but what exactly that means can vary. Some people call this "Folk Witchcraft" and assert that they are following the example of earlier witches, often those from whichever culture they came from (specifically European).

WICCAN

Witches who follow the (more or less) organized religion of Wicca. This usually includes observing the eight sabbats of the Wheel of the Year, adhering to the Wiccan Rede (a rule that in its most basic

form says, "An it harm none, do as ye will"), and belief in the Threefold Law (otherwise known as the Law of Returns: whatever you put out into the universe comes back to you times three). Gardnerian, Alexandrian, and Dianic are all forms of Wicca. There are also witches who do not consider themselves strictly Wiccan who use aspects of Wicca in their practice.

As said before, this list is only a beginning. There are more different types of Witchcraft than I could possibly include in this book. If none of the aforementioned approaches appeal to you, by all means explore the possibilities. Pretty much your only limits are your interests and your imagination.

Just as there is no one right approach to being a Witch, there is no one way to actually practice your Craft. Some people only celebrate the holidays. Others don't bother with the sabbats but do things on full and new moons. Many, but not most, cast spells either on those occasions or whenever when they feel the need. And then there are witches who integrate their practices into their daily lives and carry their Witchcraft into the garden, the kitchen, and even the bedroom. (Yes, sex magic is a thing.)

If you belong to a coven or group, you may do all or most of your Witchcraft with others. Or you may do all or most of your practicing on your own. My personal path is a mix of both; my more formal magical work is usually shared with Blue Moon Circle, but my Witchcraft beliefs are a path I walk all day every day in various different forms.

There are so many ways to practice Witchcraft that there's no way to list them all in this book. As with figuring out what kind of Witchcraft you are drawn to, I suggest doing additional exploration on your own on what practices you'd like to incorporate. In the next several chapters we will look at some of the basic and most common options.

• • • ACTIVITY 2 • • •
Which Kind of Witch?

Some people know right away which type or types of Witchcraft practice they want to follow. For others, it takes time and experimentation to figure it out. If you're just starting out, or if you've been on this road for a while but still trying to find your identity as a witch, it can be helpful to try a number of different approaches and try journaling about them to see which ones resonate with you the most.

A WORD ON THE WICCAN REDE

The Wiccan Rede (an old word meaning "counsel" or "advice") is one of the core tenets of Wicca. In its shorter form, it says: *An it harm none, do as ye will*. Without the flowery language, what it means is that you can do whatever you want as long as it doesn't hurt anyone. It can be difficult to tell which actions might actually create harm no matter how good your intentions—and don't forget that "harm none" includes yourself. So not only do you have to consider the far-reaching possibilities of whatever you do, especially when it comes to magical work, you must also consider whether your choices could have negative repercussions in your own life. This is a complicated rule, and not every witch chooses to follow it (after all, it is a Wiccan idea, and not all witches are Wiccan). Whether or not you follow it is up to you.

Chapter Three
THE SABBATS

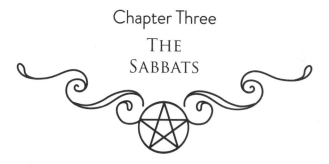

The sabbats are the eight holidays that make up the Wheel of the Year. Although the Wheel itself is a Wiccan construct, most of the holidays far predate modern Witchcraft, and many of them are celebrated in cultures across the world in various different forms.

Not all witches celebrate all eight sabbats, but for many of us these days are vital to our practice, whether we use them to worship God and Goddess, practice magic appropriate to the season, or simply as a reason to celebrate. (Or a combination of all of those things.) The sabbats are also a good way to affirm your connection to nature, since they focus on the specific energies of that time of the year. (Keep in mind that the dates are reversed in the Southern Hemisphere; when it is the winter solstice here, it is the summer solstice there.)

Imbolc

February 2. Imbolc is a quarter-cross holiday, meaning it falls midway between a solstice and an equinox. It celebrates the first stirring of spring below the earth and is the origin of the more secular Groundhog Day. It is a time to consider your goals both mundane and magical for the coming seasons and a good time to cast spells for cleansing and purification to prepare yourself for the more active part of the year. Even if it still feels like winter, there is a burgeoning sense of anticipation and energy as the days slowly lengthen, and you can tap into this to help bring yourself out of hibernation.

Spring Equinox

On or around March 21. (The dates of the equinoxes and solstices are based on solar movement, and vary by a few days year to year.) Sometimes called Ostara, this sabbat celebrates the arrival of spring, even if it doesn't always look like it outside your window. Its general focus is on new beginnings and implementing plans. A time for hope and celebration, it is only one of two days in the year (the other being the fall equinox) when darkness and light are in perfect balance, equal amounts of both. Traditionally, the holiday uses ancient Pagan symbols for fertility such as rabbits and eggs, and it is likely that much of the Christian symbolism for Easter was adopted from these earlier Pagan roots. It is common to do magical work that plants the seeds (literal and metaphorical) for longterm plans and goals or for increased balance in your life in whichever forms you might need.

Beltane

May 1. Also known as Beltaine or May Day, some witches start their celebrations on May Eve and continue them from sundown to sundown. It is based on an ancient Celtic fire festival and is a celebration of love, fertility, and passion. In some traditions, this is the day on which the Goddess and God consummate their love for each other, and it can be a blatantly sexual holiday. However, it is also a celebration of love in all its forms, and some witches choose this day for their handfastings or weddings. You can also do magical work for fertility in all its forms and to invoke or appreciate love in whichever aspect makes the most sense in your own life. This holiday may have been used in older days to bless the fields and the crops that would be growing in them, which can be applied in a less literal way to ask for success in any important endeavors.

Summer Solstice

On or about June 21. This is the longest day of the year and the shortest night. Although it is also referred to as midsummer, it is actually the first official day of summer. This holiday honors the Sun God in all his forms and is often celebrated with bonfires or other representations of the sun or fire. The summer solstice is another sabbat that is sometimes observed starting on the eve of the night before or starting at dawn and going until sunset. The

energy of the earth is at its height now, and we can tap into it for magical work that focuses on abundance, growth, and energy of our own. If you set goals at Imbolc, the summer solstice is a good time to give them a boost if they need it.

Lammas

August 1. Another quarter-cross holiday, this one is also sometimes referred to as Lughnasadh in honor of Lugh, a Celtic sun god. It is the first of three harvest festivals on the Wheel of the Year; a successful harvest was so important to our Pagan ancestors, and Lammas specifically celebrates the grain harvest. The harvest holidays are particularly nice to share with friends or family, if you can, and indulge in a feast of seasonal produce. A fresh loaf of bread, too. You can do magical work for your own successful harvest, whether actual or metaphorical, or prosperity work in general.

Mabon

On or around September 21. Mabon is a modern name for the autumn or fall equinox, the second harvest festival on our calendar. It is the other day of the year when the light and dark are equal, which makes it a great time to work on balance in your life. (Who couldn't use more of that?) Some call it the Witches' Thanksgiving, and primarily use it as a day of celebration and gratitude for the bounty in our lives. Even if things aren't going as well as you might wish, there is always plenty to be grateful for, and this sabbat is a good reminder of that.

Samhain

October 31. If that date sounds familiar, it is because many of the aspects of our modern Halloween were taken from much older Pagan traditions. It is said that the veil between the worlds of the living and those who have gone beyond are thinnest on this day, so it is little wonder that Halloween features ghosts and spooky things. In Witchcraft, many consider this to be our most sacred holiday. We use it to communicate with our beloved dead and say goodbye to those we have lost in the past year. Some consider it to be the Witch's New Year as well as the third harvest festival, and we let go of this year's burdens and look forward to whatever lies ahead in the next turning of the Wheel. It is a time for powerful ritual if you are so inclined, but you can also celebrate quietly by lighting candles to honor those who have passed through the veil or do some solitary divination work.

Yule

On or around December 21. Yule comes from the old Norse jōl, the winter solstice. This is the shortest day of the year with the most darkness and the least amount of light. But we celebrate the returning sun because moving forward, each day has a little bit more light than the one before it. Like Christmas, which took many of its traditions from older forms of this holiday, we celebrate by bringing trees and greenery inside to represent life in the midst of death, decorate with red and green for holly and mistletoe, and gather with friends and family to exchange gifts and good wishes. It is customary to light candles to represent the reappearance of the sun, and it is a good time to do magical work to increase, hope, and joy.

Feasting

Sabbats are often celebrated with a feast, especially if you have gathered with a group. These are often potlucks where everyone taking part brings a dish to contribute to the table, although sometimes whomever is hosting the event will provide all the food, in which case the others attending may chip in toward the cost. In general, the food should reflect whichever holiday you are celebrating with dishes that reflect the season, such as fresh herb salads in the spring and corn and squashes in the autumn. Of course, that's not a rule, and really you can have whatever you want. It is all about sharing food and the company of those with whom you have just created ritual. It also serves the practical task of grounding you after an intense spiritual experience. Feasts aren't just for groups, either.

If you are celebrating the sabbats on your own, you can still make a special meal to observe the holiday.

A Note on Feast Foods

Keep in mind that many people have food allergies, sensitivities, and/or special dietary needs. If you practice with the same group of people all the time (or are only creating a small feast for yourself), this may not be an issue. But if you are hosting a large group or inviting new attendees for the first time, you may want to ask ahead of time if anyone has special food issues. You can also ask those who are bringing dishes to write down a list of ingredients on a card so that those who need to avoid certain foods will know not to eat those particular items. If there is going to be a large bunch, you will probably want to make sure that some of your offerings are vegetarian, vegan, or gluten free.

Chaper Four
THE LUNAR CYCLE

While almost all witches practice on the night of the full moon, some also do magical work throughout the entire lunar cycle. The moon represents the Goddess, and as the moon waxes and wanes, its energy shifts and changes as well. Different lunar phases are thought to represent the different forms of the Goddess—Maiden, Mother, and Crone—as well as having varying types of energy that are naturally suitable for different kinds of magical work.

This doesn't mean you can't do spells or other magic on any night of the month. What it does mean is that you may want to give some thought to what kinds of work you plan so that you can benefit from the natural energies available to you at the time. You can—and I do—cast a spell that you need *right now* regardless of the moon cycle. But if you have the flexibility to do so, it is not a bad idea to go with the flow of the moon's phases.

One of the great things about moon magic is that it doesn't matter where you live. Urban Witches and Rural Witches all see the same beautiful orb in the night sky. Obviously, it is nice if you can stand outside and gaze up at her, but even if you can't, the energy is there just the same.

Dark Moon/New Moon

Usually lasting about three days, the dark moon is the phase when the moon cannot be seen at all. The new moon, astronomically speaking, is the middle one of those days, when the moon is exactly between waxing and waning. Most witches use these terms interchangeably, although some witches consider the new moon to be the point when the tiniest crescent of the moon can again be seen in the sky. Some witches don't do magical work during the dark moon at all, using it as a time of rest and regeneration. Others use it for divination or dream work, although it is useful for banishing. The new moon is often used for new beginnings or self-exploration. This time is considered to belong to the Goddess in her aspect as Crone.

Waxing Moon

This is the phase between the new moon and the full moon, where the moon grows larger every day. It is generally used for magical work for *increase*, or more of something. For instance, if you are having money problems, you could do prosperity spells that ask the Goddess to send you a better job, unexpected gifts, or some sort of lucky windfall. This is a good time to ask for better health, more love in your life, and so on. This time is said to belong to the Goddess in her Maiden form. Popular Witchcraft author Dorothy Morrison refers to the Waxing Moon Goddess as the "Light Maiden" and the Waning Moon Goddess as the "Dark Maiden." *[Everyday Moon Magic: Spells & Rituals for Abundant Living. Llewellyn, 2003.]*

Full Moon

The most powerful part of the lunar cycle, and arguably the Witch's favorite night of the month, is the full moon.

Most witches consider this to be not only the actual night when the moon is at it fullest, but also the day before and the day after. The moon's energy is at its height and it is the perfect time to do magical work that requires an extra boost or is very important. This is also the night when a group of witches is most likely to gather, to take advantage of the available energy and connect with the Goddess in her aspect as Mother. But you don't need to be in a coven to connect to the Goddess. Simply walk outside and gaze up at the sky, opening yourself to the energy of the moon that represents the very heart of our Craft.

Waning Moon

The waning moon is the phase between the full and dark moon, as its crescent slowly becomes smaller and smaller. This phase is generally used for magical work for decrease, or the lessening of something. So instead of doing a spell to bring in more prosperity, for instance, you might do one to lessen debt, or rid yourself of bad habits, or ease health issues. You can have the exact same purpose (prosperity, healing, love, etc.), it is simply the approach that changes.

Lunar Eclipses

A lunar eclipse occurs when the moon moves into the earth's shadow. For this to happen, the earth, moon, and sun must be aligned with the earth in the middle, and it only occurs when the moon is full. Since this is a relatively rare event, it is considered to be a very powerful time for magical work. Lunar eclipses can be total or partial, but they are all special. You can think of it as a rare conjunction of lunar and solar energies, and use it for important magical work or simply bathe in the potential for change it brings.

Blue Moon

There are two different kinds of blue moons, both of which can be viewed as magical. Technically, a blue moon is the third full moon in a season that has four full moons. This happens about every three years. But due to incorrect information printed in an article in 1946, most people believe that a blue moon is the second full moon in one month, which has become the general usage. Most witches go by the second, more common definition. This phenomenon can be treated the same as any other full moon, or you can do some kind of special magical work that you wouldn't normally to, to celebrate its unusual occurrence.

Fun fact

We named our coven "Blue Moon Circle" because when we first started, there were only three of us, and while we invited others to join us for sabbats, we did full moons by ourselves. Since we had such a small number of people, if one of us couldn't make it, we usually cancelled. So we only got together every once in a blue moon. Hence the name!

Chapter Five
SPECIAL OCCASIONS

Besides the seasonal and lunar cycles, there are a few special occasions when witches might gather together. There are certain times when it is important to celebrate with your spiritual community, if you are fortunate enough to have one. Not that you need an excuse. Feel free to hold a weekly witchy margarita and movies night, if that's the way you roll!

Wiccaning/Baby Blessing

If you're a Wiccan, this is usually referred to as a "Wiccaning" (to parallel the Christian "christening" version), but it is essentially a New Child Blessing event, and you can certainly call it that if you prefer. Unlike a christening, which officially makes the child a part of that religion, a Wiccaning or Child Blessing simply welcomes the new child to the community and celebrates their birth.

A Wiccaning/Child Blessing may happen soon after a baby is born, or whenever the parent or parents feel comfortable. It can also be used for any new child, including one who is adopted into a family. There is no set format for this type of ritual. Usually a community or group leader will introduce the parents and the child, although the parents can do it themselves. Gifts are given but are often metaphorical; for example, individuals may step forward and bless the child with "a bright future," "a love of learning," or "a healthy life." Actual gifts may be given as well. It can be done inside a formal ritual setting, if that is the way your group tends to do things, or it can be less formal.

Sometimes non-witch family members and friends are invited if they would be comfortable doing so. It is an occasion of great joy, and therefore there is almost always

A Note on Raising Witchy Children

Witches believe in free will and that everyone must make the choice of religion or spiritual path for themselves. So while parents may raise their children with Pagan or Witchcraft traditions, the children are free to make their own choice of what they believe when old enough to do so.

a feast afterward. It is optional to have "goddess-parents" step forward and pledge to help guide and help the child as they grow and learn.

Handfasting

A handfasting is a Pagan wedding ceremony. Handfastings may be done for a year and a day, which is a traditional Wiccan time period (most levels of training take a year and a day, for instance), or for life. Some couples say, "As long as love lasts" in their vows, giving themselves the freedom to dissolve the binding if their love fades.

Handfastings can certainly be legally binding ceremonies depending on who performs them and what the couple desires. The officiant can be a nondenominational minister, a Justice of the Peace, or a high priest or priestess. For non-legal handfastings, the officiant's title doesn't matter beyond the couple's preference.

There are numerous traditional elements that can be included in a handfasting ritual, including jumping the broom (in which the couple jumps over a broom together to signify that they are starting a new life as one home), lighting a unity candle (using two smaller separate candles to light a larger one in unison), drinking out of a shared goblet, and the aforementioned tying together of hands (the ribbon or ties used for this are usually considered a treasured keepsake and kept in a special pouch or box).

Handfastings are an option for those who want a more witchy ceremony or wish to commit to each other without the legal trappings, or those who may not be able to marry legally (or publicly) due to societal constraints. It is a celebration of love in whichever forms it takes. Sometimes non-witchy folks are invited, sometimes not, depending on the circumstances.

I have performed many handfastings in my time, but my favorite was for my coven-mate Robin and her husband, who is "Pagan-friendly" and happy to have me officiate. I got certified as a non-denominational minister so that the marriage would be legal, and the three of us collaborated to create a ritual that would have the witchy elements that were important to Robin while keeping them subtle enough that they wouldn't offend the parents of either the bride or the groom, who came from more conventional religious backgrounds. The chairs were set in a circle a few rows deep, and the flower girl walked around the outside scattering rose petals, closing the circle after both the bride and groom had entered.

No one outside of us knew that a magical circle had just been cast. The quarters were cast using a poem that was not obviously Pagan, and we referred to "a power greater than us" rather than specifically to Goddess and God. After they exchanged vows and rings, I read aloud a blessing that had been handed out to all those attending so that they could join in blessing the couple as well.

Next was a hand-fastening, then the lighting of a unity candle, and then a drink shared from a goblet. These more witchy elements were explained as traditional in part of the program handed out to each of the guests when they arrived. The ceremony was moving and powerful, and it satisfied the desires of everyone involved. Magic indeed.

Croning/Eldering

In today's world, getting older is mostly seen as a bad thing. Women are expected to dye their hair and lie about their ages. Some people have surgery or go to other extreme lengths to keep looking young. And while there is nothing wrong with doing what you can to stay healthy and energetic, there is something to be said for appreciating the wisdom and experience that come with the years and a life well-lived, no matter your age.

Witches and Pagans generally tend to have respect for the elders of our community, whether leaders, teachers, or just the person standing next to us during ritual. Since

Witchcraft as a whole tends to be made up of people who look and act different from the average, it has been my experience that witches are usually less likely to pass judgments on each other based on appearance or lifestyle (although there are always some—don't be one of the "some," I'm just saying).

In Witchcraft, being called a crone is not an insult. After all, even our Goddess has her crone phase (and some might say that the crone goddesses, such as Hecate, are pretty kick-ass). In addition, because we are a fairly new religion, albeit based in some ways on a much older one, we don't actually have very many elders. Teachers and mentors are a valuable resource, so it behooves us to treat them with the honor and respect they deserve.

While the word "crone" refers to a woman who has reached a certain age (a number that varies widely depending on your definition and a woman's perception of herself), an elder can be any gender; if a woman isn't comfortable with the term "crone," she can certainly call herself an elder instead.

A woman may have a Croning/Eldering ceremony when she reaches menopause, or when her children leave home and she moves from the mother stage of her life into the

crone years. This can be a major shift in focus (inward rather than outward) for some women/those who identify as mothers. Anyone regardless of gender might celebrate their retirement, or moving into a position as an elder or teacher in the Witchcraft community. There is no right or wrong time or way to observe this rite of passage. It is completely dependent on the person for whom the Eldering is held.

Some people prefer to lead their own ritual with friends and loved ones invited to bear witness. It can also be done as a solitary, by and for themselves. Otherwise, the ceremony is usually led by a group leader (if the person is in a coven), local high priest or high priestess, or someone else who feels comfortable doing it. The ritual may be reserved for the person's magical community, or they may choose to invite non-witches who would be accepting of the idea.

Passing Over

A Passing Over ritual is a Witchcraft version of a funeral. Pagans in general tend to have a somewhat different view of death than others in our society do. While it is always sad to lose someone, death is viewed as a part of the natural cycle of life: birth, life, death, and rebirth. Many witches believe that when someone dies, they go to a place called the Summerlands to rest and recharge and be reunited with loved ones. Many of us also believe in reincarnation and that each of us will eventually return to this plane to continue learning and growing, in a cycle as natural as the waxing and waning of the moon.

A belief in reincarnation doesn't mean that those who have passed to the other side aren't mourned; a Passing Over ceremony is a celebration of the person's life and how they touched the lives and hearts of those left behind. The ritual serves to create a safe place for loved ones to share memories, tell stories, and come together in remembrance and appreciation. There may be an altar where people can place pictures or keepsakes that represent something about the person who has died, and individuals may choose to light a candle and speak directly to the departed one, who might well be present and listening. A Passing Over ritual can also be held for a beloved pet.

Rebirthing Ritual

It is not unusual for a person to go through a major shift at some point in their life, something that so changes them and the way they view the world that it is important to note and celebrate it. We have celebrations for the day we were born, after all. Why not do the same for someone who has gone through a life-altering event and feels as though they have been reborn?

Rebirthing is a way of honoring your new self and the strength it took to make whatever major change it brought about. It doesn't matter what the change is, although it should be saved for something major. Some people do a rebirthing when they get divorced or leave a long-term destructive relationship, when they finally overcome addiction or illness, come out of the closet or transition, or retire after a lifetime of hard work. Whatever the reason, the Rebirthing is a way to affirm both to yourself and rest of the world (or whoever you choose to include in the ceremony) that you are a reborn, new you, and you embrace that identity with joy. You can also do this as a solitary ritual, if you prefer.

Initiations

When a witch joins a coven, they sometimes take part in an initiation ceremony to officially make them a part of the group. This was common with traditional Wiccan covens, though many modern and less formal eclectic covens are less likely to do so. Although there were specific rituals for initiations in Gardnerian or Alexandrian Wicca, for instance, these days a coven can design a ceremony to suit their particular needs or style, or skip it altogether.

Dedication

A dedication is slightly different from an initiation. When we formed Blue Moon Circle, we did a group dedication to formalize our commitment to each other and to the coven. However, anyone joining after that initial time wasn't asked to do an initiation of any kind, and we didn't redo the dedication when we added new members. One might also do what is called a self-dedication (meaning a Solitary Witch would perform a ritual, rather than having one led by a priest or priestess). Some witches do a self-dedication to commit themselves to the Craft or to a particular god/dess. When I became a high priestess, I did a small dedication ritual with the help of two friends in which I dedicated myself to the service of the gods in general and the Pagan community as a whole.

Chapter Six
DAILY PRACTICES

Witchcraft isn't just about holidays, full moons, and special occasions, as wonderful as those are. For many, it is a way of life. It is how you walk your talk, the spiritual beliefs that guide your choices from the time you get up in the morning until the time you go to bed at night. It is about connecting with nature, connecting to deity, connecting to your own inner wisdom, and connecting to others who share at least some of your beliefs. It is about magic. We are witches all day every day, although how that manifests is different for everyone. Here are some of the many possibilities.

Kitchen Witchery

One of my favorite ways to integrate Witchcraft into my daily life is by adding a little magic to cooking. It is something I am doing anyway, so it doesn't take any extra time or effort (not much, anyway). Mostly it is about adding a little extra focus and intent as you prepare your food, and maybe being more purposeful in choosing specific ingredients. For instance, say you need to do some prosperity work and were already planning to make a casserole for dinner. Simply add some vegetables and herbs associated with prosperity magic (see the Correspondences section for helpful lists) and focus on your intention to draw in more abundance as you mix and stir the ingredients.

Many books can help you integrate magic into your cooking, including fun cookbooks. One of my go-to's is *Cunningham's Encyclopedia of Wicca in the Kitchen*.

Many of the herbs in your kitchen are the same as the herbs you would use for magical work, which makes it even easier to do Kitchen Witchery! Try keeping some or all of the following in your spice cabinet: basil, cinnamon, dill, garlic, oregano, parsley, peppermint, rosemary, sage, thyme.

• • • ACTIVITY 3 • • •
Cooking with Magic

Take one of your favorite recipes and see how you can tweak it to be a little more magical. Check out the ingredients and see if any of them lend themselves to a particular type of magic, or if you can add a few herbs and spices to make it do so. Or even better, create a recipe from scratch with a magical intention, such as healing, love, prosperity, or peace.

Growing Plants

Whether you are a Garden Witch with a dozen raised beds filled with vegetables, or an Urban Witch with a few pots of herbs on your windowsill, growing something green (or pink, or yellow) is a great way to connect to nature on a regular basis. Putting your hands in the dirt can be very grounding—pun intended—and practical as well, if you eat what you grow or use it in your magical work. There is also something to be said for plants that are beautiful, even if they have no other purpose, since they raise our spirits and gladden our hearts. Some indoor plants even clean the air. As with cooking, making growing things magical is mostly a matter of being mindful, although even if you aren't thinking about it, you are still connecting with the power of the element of earth.

· · · ACTIVITY 4 · · ·
Planting Herbs

Plant a few herbs that you intend to use for Kitchen Witchery or some other magic. Be mindful as you put the soil into a container or prepare the ground in your garden. When you put the seeds into the dirt, focus on your intention to use them for positive magical work, and send them energy for growth and power. Don't forget to check in on them periodically as they grow and renew that energy and intention from time to time.

If you only have space for a few herbs, try these multipurpose ones: basil, dill, parsley, mint, rosemary, and lavender.

Creating Altars and Sacred Space

Depending on your living situation, you may choose to decorate your home with all sorts of witchy items, put up a small subtle altar, or create sacred space in ways that aren't necessarily obvious to others. I live by myself and am obviously firmly out of the broom closet, so I have altars in my living room, dining room, and bedroom (that one's dedicated to the cats I've lost), as well as a permanent stone circle out back behind my barn, in addition to brooms, black cats, and other witchy symbols all over the house.

If you share your home with others who aren't witches, or if you might have guests who would disapprove (and you're not out of the broom closet yet), or even if you simply choose not to go overboard, there are still various different ways you can make the place you live in a witchy haven. If you are free to decorate in any way you wish, here are some suggestions for creating a magical environment in and around your home.

Altars

An altar is basically a table or shelf that serves as a focal point for worship, ritual, and magical work. In some cultures, in is common to have a family altar devoted to

THE SUBTLE ALTAR

An altar doesn't have to be obvious to serve its purpose. For instance, the symbols of the elements (e.g., a feather, a candle, a rock, and a shell) can be found in many homes. You could use a chalice, small iron cauldron, or even a bowl to represent the Goddess; for the God you could use a stick or antler, or a decorative letter opener instead of an athame. You're the only one who has to know what those things stand for and that they aren't simply decorative! Witchcraft doesn't have to be obvious.

your ancestors. In others, the household altar might be dedicated to a particular deity or deities. Witches may have these types of altars, but they also are likely to have ones with a more general witchy theme. For instance, an altar might have statues of a god and goddess, things that symbolize the four elements (such as a feather for air, a candle for fire, a stone for earth, and a shell for water), crystals, ritual candles, an athame, and so on. An altar is a completely personal space that you can set up in any way you desire. You can also set up an altar for a ritual or spellwork and then put it away again.

· · · ACTIVITY 5 · · ·
Creating a Portable Altar

This is an altar that you can use to perform magical work anywhere you are, whether it is hidden away most of the time in your own home, taken to a meeting place outside or at someone else's house, or carried along on trips. This can be as simple or as fancy as you desire. Start with a nice box or bag you can pack everything into. Then you'll need a pretty, lightweight cloth to spread everything out on when you set up the altar. You may want to include some or all of the following items, depending on your style of practice: mini candles with small holders (you may want these in the quarter colors of red, yellow, green, and blue, plus a few extras for whatever magical work you'll be doing, or you might use all white), candles for the Goddess and God, incense or cleansing herbs, a small vial of salt and water, chalk for drawing symbols or a toothpick for etching into the candles, and a small piece of parchment paper and a pen for writing down spells. Don't forget the matches! It can also be helpful to have a compass in case you need to find the directions.

Circles

A circle is the space within which ritual is held. Many times this is a temporary magical construct, which is cast by an individual or a group of witches just for the time of the actual ritual. Some witches, however, have permanent circles, like the traditional nine-foot stone circle out behind my barn. You don't necessarily have to build anything. Just reserve a space for magical work and keep it mowed or otherwise neat. Or plant flowers in a circle. Like an altar, your circle can be as simple or as complicated as you like. One clever way to have a permanent circle that no one else knows about is to use a throw rug. You can either draw the circle, and any magical symbols you like, on the floor, and then cover it up with the rug, or you can draw on the underside of the rug itself. Chalk will do fine if you don't want to use pen or paint. You know it is there, but no one else will.

Sacred Space

Sacred space is any place where you create magic or practice spiritual work on a regular basis (although you create temporary sacred space every time you cast a circle, I'm talking in this case about a more permanent fixture). For a Garden Witch, their garden may be sacred space, even though it looks to the outside eye as though it is simply a place to grow peas and lettuce. They may bless and consecrate the garden area when they create it or first start using it for magical work. Or it may simply take on the energy of sacred space after repeated use. I know witches who have built their own small labyrinths, or who dedicate a room in their house for magical use. Sacred space is wherever you create it.

Housework

You might not have considered housework as a way to integrate magic into your daily life, but like cooking, it is something that most of us do all the time (well, okay, some of the time) anyway, and it is actually quite easy to

LEAVE THE
WORLD BEHIND

A friend taught me this great trick years ago. It only takes a minute and it really works. Put a bowl of water near where you enter your house, along with a small towel. If you want, you can put a clear quartz crystal in the bottom of the bowl. Whenever you come in from spending time in the outside world, dip your hands into the water and visualize any negativity or unpleasantness draining away into the bowl. Don't be surprised if you need to change the water periodically, because it ends up getting kind of nasty from all that ick you're washing away.

add a magical spin to the things you are already doing. For instance, if you are going to sweep, you can spritz your broom with some magical cleansing oils before you start, and then visualize sweeping away negative energy (left-over from stress or arguments, for instance, or that visit from your cranky Aunt Gladys) as you move through the various spaces of your home. If you can, sweep it right out the door, although you can always visualize it. You can do the same thing while you are dusting or mopping.

· · · ACTIVITY 6 · · ·
Spiritual Spring Cleaning

While it is nice to do this in the spring to get a fresh start on the year, you can do it whenever you feel the need. I also like to do a deep clean in autumn, since I know I will be heading into a long, cold winter when I'll be stuck inside my house for most of the time. That's a little more pleasant when the energy of your home feels clear and clean. The difference between regular cleaning and spiritual cleaning is all in the focus and intention, so before you begin, take a few minutes to ground yourself and sit with the intention of clearing away any negativity, stagnant energy, or problem spots in your home. Once you are ready, do the following:

1. If the weather allows, open at least one window in each room. Starting at the top of the house (or toward the back, if you only have one story), light your favorite cleansing herbs or incense (I like to use a sage bundle if it is ethically sourced, but there are numerous options) and walk through each room. Slowly waft the smoke around the room, paying special attention to any place that allows entrance or exit, such as doors, windows, chimneys, and so on. Visualize the herbs or incense cleansing the energy of the room, and anything you don't want going out the window (even if it isn't open). Close the windows as you leave each room. Finish up at the door used to enter and exit the house most often, and open it briefly to allow the last of the unwanted energy to leave. If you wish, you can call on the elements of fire and air to help you.

2. Repeat the above with a mixture of salt and water (sea salt is best but regular will do if it's all you have): move through each room and sprinkle the mixture into corners and

around the spaces where anything feels stuck or muddled. If you wish, you can call on the elements of earth and water to help you.

3. If it feels as though there are particularly stubborn issues or lingering darkness in the atmosphere, go through the house again with a bell, rattle, or some other instrument you can ring or shake. The vibrations will help to cleanse the area.

When you are done, you may want to renew any protection magic you have around the house, to help it stay cleansed and clear as long as possible, and thank the elements if you called on them to help you.

Bathing and Cleansing Yourself

Just as you can add a magical touch to your housecleaning with the use of intention and visualization, you can also do the same for yourself. The fastest and easiest way to do this is by adding a small ritual to your shower. Either as you are soaping up and rinsing off, or afterward, visualize anything you don't want being washed away and swirling down the drain. You can imagine the soap and shampoo or the water itself are glowing with a magical light. If

ALTAR ATTENTION

When you are doing spiritual cleaning, don't forget to pay attention to your altar if you have one. After all, it is one of the most sacred places in your home, and it is insulting to the God/dess to let it get too messy. A couple of times a year at least, take everything off your altar, dust and clean it, and then put everything back, maybe changing things around to reflect the season or what you are focusing on in your life. Do this with mindfulness and reverence, and send gratitude to whatever deity you worship when finished.

you want, you can say something simple, like "Stress and pain, go down the drain, leave me feeling good again" (or whatever words seem right to you.) If you want to do something more focused and powerful, you can add in a body wash made with herbs that you have consecrated for magical work, or take a magic bath, if you are lucky enough to have a tub.

If you are using essential oils, you only need a few drops. If you are going to use fresh or dried herbs, you will probably want to put them into some kind of bag—I like the little muslin drawstring ones—so you won't have a mess to clean up when you're done.

· · · Activity 7 · · ·
Bathing Bliss

If you have a bathtub, you can literally immerse yourself in cleansing, healing magic. Try to find some time when you won't be interrupted. Make sure you leave the phone in another room! Gather up a few simple ingredients such as sea salt (Epsom salts will work too, especially if you have pain issues), essential oils or herbs good for healing and cleansing (for a relaxing bath, try rose petals, lavender, lemon balm, and/or chamomile. For a more cleansing bath I like rosemary; peppermint; and orange, lemon, or grapefruit essential oils, but you can use any herbs you like), and you can even put a few crystals in the bottom of the tub. If it is safe to do so, light a couple of candles. As you focus on cleansing and healing, run the water for your bath and add your salt and herbs. Then sit in the tub and relax, feeling the magic work its way into every pore.

Easy Daily Protection Work

We live in a world that for many feels increasingly dangerous and full of unpleasant circumstances and people. Luckily there are a few simple mini-rituals we can do for protection on a daily basis or whenever we feel the need. For instance, to protect your home, whenever you take a shower, draw a pentacle or whatever symbols you feel are protective in the steam on a window or mirror. If you are in a situation where you need a little boost of protection, take a moment to visualize yourself surrounded by a bubble of bright light full of God/dess energy. If you want, you can also imagine the outside of the bubble is a mirror that reflects any negative energy back to wherever it is coming from.

CAR KARMA

When you are doing protection work, don't forget your vehicle, if you have one. You can do all sorts of things to give your car, truck, motorcycle, or invisible plane a little bit of added magical protection when you take it out into the world. You can bless and consecrate it as you would any other tool and space. You can tuck a protection amulet into the glove compartment or under a seat. Protective signs and sigils can be drawn with your finger on the hood, top, rear, and sides (with or without water)—or you can even write them in the dirt and pollen if your car is a bit dusty!

Chapter Seven
WITCHY CRAFTS

I f you are a crafty witch (and many of us are), you can celebrate your witchiness and channel magic through various different types of arts or crafts. Believe it or not, this is actually traditional: many early witches, especially women, probably worked their magic with everyday items they created for practical use, from the brooms they used to sweep floors to the clothing they wove or sewed for their families.

There are many different approaches to integrating Witchcraft into crafting, so don't worry if you're not a master at pottery or a gifted painter. Remember too that it is less about perfection than about the intent you are putting into whatever you're creating. Here are a few simple possibilities, although if you do some form of crafting that isn't mentioned here, I am sure you can figure out ways to integrate magic into whatever you do.

What makes regular craft work magical? You start with a clear intention, and focus on that as you create whatever it is you are making. You might even say a spell beforehand, or bless and consecrate a finished item.

··· SPELL 1 ···
Crafting Spell

Here is a simple spell you can say when you start a project: "Let my Craft make this craft magical. May my hands be skilled and my power true and strong. So mote it be." (You can substitute the name of the specific craft you are doing and add your intention, such as "for prosperity" if you wish.)

Sewing

Although not as fast and efficient as using a machine, sewing by hand gives you a chance to stitch magic into whatever you are making. It might be something overtly magical, like a poppet created for healing, or it might be more subtle, like stitching symbols for protection into the inside of a loved one's jacket. Or sewing the rune Gifu (which looks like an X) inside your wallet to draw prosperity and gifts. Focus on your intention with every stitch. If you want, you can repeat the word for your magical intention over and over.

··· ACTIVITY 8 ···
Charm Bags and Magic Sachets

One of the easiest and most widely used forms of craft magic is the charm bag or magical sachet. To create one, you take a square or rectangle of cloth and sew up three of the four sides. Once you have your bag, place the ingredients for your spell inside—for instance, if you are making a charm bag for prosperity, you might use herbs like basil, cinnamon, and peppermint, along with a tumbled stone like aventurine or malachite, along with anything else you are using (I like to include a piece of paper with the spell written on it along with some runes or other symbols). If you are making a charm bag, you will  tie it closed with ribbon, string, or thread. If you are making a sachet, then you will sew the fourth side shut. Tuck it in a pocket, under your pillow, or place it on your altar.

Fiber Arts

All fiber arts lend themselves well to magical work. This includes things like knitting, crocheting, or weaving, in addition to needlework, cross-stitching, and embroidery. These crafts can be powerful tools for magical work because of their repetitive nature. With every movement, you can whisper your goal or simply focus on it silently as you work, so the magic becomes a part of whatever object you are creating.

Jewelry

Many witches wear magical jewelry, often adorned with crystals or pentacles. These can be obvious, but if you want to be more subtle, you can string magical intentions along with gemstone beads or even pretty glass ones.

Clay

Clay is malleable and can be crafted into many different shapes with assorted different purposes. You can make bowls or plates to use during rituals (limit anything used with food to those coated with something food-safe), pendants can be made into jewelry, or magical items to hang around the house. My first high priestess was a professional potter with a kiln, so the members of our coven were each able to make our own set of rune stones that she then fired for us. Blue Moon Circle has a member who spent years as a potter too, and she helped us create the large goblet we use for "cakes and ale" during rituals. She shaped the goblet, then we each took a turn decorating it with colored glazes we could use to paint symbols or pictures with. She took it home, covered it with a clear coating, and fired it. Once it was done, we blessed and consecrated it and have been using it ever since.

If you don't happen to have a kiln handy, use self-drying clay instead.

· · · ACTIVITY 9 · · ·
Decorative Plaques

With a flat piece of clay and a pointed tool to etch it with, you can craft a plaque to lay on your altar or hang on the wall. Most of these are simply decorative, but if you have a specific magical goal in mind, such as protection for your home, you can easily create one that has purpose as well as beauty. Start by shaping the clay into a round, oval, square, or rectangle. If you are going to hang it, poke a hole at the top. If you are artistic, you may want to add lots of fancy detailing. If you're not, you may wish to keep it simple; perhaps a pentacle with the Tree of Life or a house with a heart inside it. Whatever you choose to etch into your clay, do it with feeling. You can also use some paints, if they work with the material.

Wax

Like clay, wax can be shaped and manipulated into many forms. The most common use, especially by us witchy types, is in candles. Most of us use store-bought candles, either generic or ones specifically designed for magical use. It is surprisingly easy to make your own at home by melting wax over a double-boiler and pouring it into molds (although a lot of fun, it can be messy). If you don't

WAX TABLETS

Just as you can paint or etch on clay (as described above), you can also do the same sort of thing using wax instead. A wax tablet can be formed into any shape or size you want, and either kept as a decorative or power item on your altar, or melted down as a part of your ritual. For instance, if you are having a problem with something, you can etch a word or symbol representing that into some wax, and melt it as part of a banishing spell. Wax is an extremely flexible medium, and you can add decorations with colored candle drippings.

want to go to that extreme, you can still add your own magical touch to premade candles by etching symbols or words into them, anointing them with magical oils (carefully avoiding the wick, since many oils are flammable), or softening the bottom third and rolling it in herbs. You can make candles for specific spells, either as part of a ritual or ahead of time. Some people like to match the candle color to the purpose (such as blue for healing) and others would rather use plain beeswax because it is more natural. You can also create magical items out of wax, either to keep or to melt down during a spell.

Wood

Witches have used wood throughout the centuries; it is a part of nature, individual types of wood are thought to have their own individual magical associations, and it has often been readily available and free. You can decorate wooden boxes to hold your tarot and oracle cards, or to store other magical tools in. Some people glue things onto the lid or sides, others paint or draw on them, or if you're handy, you can use a wood-burning tool to etch designs or symbols into the wood itself. Wood can also be used to make runes, by cutting a long stick or dowel into equal sized pieces. Blue Moon Circle used a thin but sturdy nearly straight five-foot branch to create a group staff for ritual use. We tied on feathers and interesting witchy-looking dangles with string, drew on it with colorful markers, and used flexible wire to bind a cool crystal to the top. Then we each wrote some of the things we liked about another member onto a length of ribbon and attached those so they hung down about half the length of the branch. Then we blessed and consecrated it. It was a fun project, and in the end, we had a useful tool. You can use a smaller piece of found wood and do much the same things (or something much less complicated) to make a speaking stick to pass around the circle at the end of a ritual if you happen to work with others in a group.

· · · ACTIVITY 10 · · ·
Magic Wands

You can make your own magic wand out of a piece of found wood, too. If you go for the simple approach, you don't have to do much more than remove any stray bits of bark until it is relatively smooth and possibly anoint it with magical oil. You could also use a piece of copper or silver wire to tie a clear quartz or amethyst crystal to the top. Draw, paint, or carve any symbols onto the stick, such as suns, moons, pentacles, stars, rune signs, or your

No trees on your property? Walk in a park that has some, or stroll through a neighborhood where trees line the street. After a windy day, you'll likely find fallen branches scattered on the ground.

magical name (if you have one). The only thing that matters is that it feels right to you, and comfortable for use during your spellwork.

Paper

Did you know that you could make paper at home? It's not even difficult, although it can be a little messy. (It's a great project to do with kids, if you have them and are raising them to be little witches.) You can find instructions online, but basically you take old scrap paper, rip it into tiny pieces, soak it overnight, then put it into a blender with water and lay it out on an old screen to dry. The fun part for us witchy types is that you can write magical words or intentions onto the paper scraps first or add seeds before drying it, making it so that you can actually plant your magical wishes later. How cool is that? Store-bought paper can be used for all sorts of other crafty purposes, including creating your own Book of Shadows, homemade tarot or oracle cards, or decorating pages in some special way so that you have magical

chapter seven

paper ready for those really important spells. Because paper is relatively fragile, it is a good format to use when you want to send a spell or wish out into the universe. You can burn it, or tear it up, or bury it in the ground to break up over time. You can even fold it into a paper boat and float it down a stream!

Music

You may not think of music as a form of magic, but when used with intention, it truly can be. Music is incredibly versatile. It can be used to soothe, or excite, or arouse. Musical instruments have been used in spiritual ceremonies in every culture in the world throughout history, from drums to flutes to Gregorian chants. What is a hymn but music dedicated to a religious purpose? You may already have your own favorite way of integrating music and magic but if not, you might want to give one of these a try.

- Chanting—The human voice is probably the most commonly used instrument of them all. It's free, easy to carry, and we all have one. It is true that not everyone is a spectacular singer, but I assure you that the gods don't care if you are out of tune (and if you're singing with a group of others, they won't either). You can lift your voice in joy, or sorrow, or to ask for what you need. I'm particularly fond of some of the better-known witchy chants that repeat goddess names, or connect us with the elements. Chanting with others can be incredibly powerful and moving. At the first ritual I ever went to, everyone sang a classic four-line chant. It doesn't look like much written on the page, but when you have twenty or thirty or fifty people all chanting it at once, it will raise the hair on the back of your neck with its power.

- Drumming—After singing, drumming is probably the oldest and most common form of spiritual music making. The earliest drums were made out of hides, wood, and clay, and were believed to have been used for ritualistic purposes. Since that time, they have been used in places as far-reaching as Asia and Africa to Greece and Rome. They are also important in several Native American cultures. Drums have a long history of being used for rituals and shamanic work, and modern witches have continued that tradition. They can be used for trancework, journeying, and healing, as well as celebration. Drumming can be a soothing background for meditation or guided relaxation, or its rhythmic beat can be used to generate energy within ritual to power a spell. Drums can vary from small and simple to ornate and expensive, but the best thing about them is that virtually anyone can play them. Lessons aren't needed, and while it helps if you can keep a beat, I've been in plenty of ritual circles where there were one or two strong drummers and the rest of us just did the best we could. You can also drum on your own. Or if you really don't feel comfortable doing it, there are many New Age and witchy drumming albums you can listen to.

- Other Instruments—There are plenty of other instruments that can be used during ritual or to create background music for meditation and other spiritual practices. Flutes are common due to their haunting sound, and a simple recorder can be learned fairly quickly. Anyone can use a rattle or other simple percussion instrument (seriously, if you bang two sticks together, you're doing it). Some people use bells or gongs or chimes. No matter your level of musical skill, there is something out there that should add a lift to your magical practice.

- Speaking of albums, there are a number of fabulous witchy music groups who put out albums with chants or original songs. It is worth checking out YouTube, Spotify, or your local New Age store if you have one to find one that inspires, entertains, or helps you with rituals.

· · · ACTIVITY 11 · · ·
Don't Get Rattled

It is easy to make yourself a simple, homemade rattle or shaker. Traditionally, numerous cultures have used dried and hollowed-out gourds filled with dried beans or pebbles. You can grow your own gourd or buy one when they're in season. Cut off the top or poke a hole large enough to pull out the seeds and fibrous material. Once it has dried (it may take a few months), you can fill it with dried beans or pebbles, and cover the hole or use it as a place to attach a handle. Alternatively, you can use a hollow wooden tube, an empty can with a lid, or any other container that allows you to add the rattle material inside and then close it up again. Once you've made your rattle, you can decorate it with witchy symbols, or simply use it as is.

WITCHY MUSIC

Here are a few of my favorite witchy singers and groups (among many others): Wendy Rule, Gabrielle Roth, Heather Alexander, Sharon Knight, and Daughters of Gaia.

Chapter Eight
DIVINATION

Witches use many forms of divination to tap into both their inner wisdom and knowledge from outside themselves. Some people have strong natural psychic abilities, while others use various tools to help them. Or both. If you are just starting out and experimenting with divination, it can be interesting to try out a number of different approaches to see which one most resonates with you.

For instance, some people find tarot cards too complicated and prefer rune stones, where others feel that rune
stones are too simplistic for them to get the answers they
want. If you are drawn to one tool in particular, by all
means use it, but don't be afraid to try multiple options.
After all, part of being a witch is learning and growing,
and that often means using trial and error until you figure
out what works for you best.

Some witches only do divination on special occasions,
like specific sabbats and full moons. Others have some
form of daily practice, such as pulling a tarot or oracle
card or a rune stone to gain insight or inspiration for the
day ahead. And then there are those who simply use divination when they feel the need, when they are in crisis,
or if a question arises for which they want input. (This
can be anything from, "Should I take this trip?" to "Can

this person be trusted?") There is no wrong
approach. Others aren't comfortable with
divination or don't have an aptitude for it,
and that's okay too.

But if you do want to try using divination
in your Witchcraft practice, here are some of
the many options you can try.

Tarot

Tarot is one of the most commonly used divination tools, and there are literally thousands of different decks to choose from, with more coming out every year. Many of them have stunningly beautiful artwork, so that some people collect them for that alone. You are sure to find one that resonates with you if you look long enough. One classic deck is the Rider-Waite-Smith, and many of the more modern decks (including my *Everyday Witch Tarot*) are based on the seventy-eight cards in that deck, like the Fool, the Tower, the Empress, and so on. Other decks take a completely independent approach and bear no resemblance to anything familiar. Some people find the tarot difficult to master, so it can be helpful to have someone with more experience teach you if that is an option. But many witches simply learn by practicing and reading the guidebooks that come with whichever deck they chose. (Note: some guidebooks are very basic and not all that helpful, so you might want to check out the book *and* the deck before you buy if you think you're going to need more detail.) While people do sometimes pull one card for a simple answer (usually yes or no), tarot cards are usually used in what are called spreads, which are various layouts. These can be as simple as the three-card spread, which is often past/present/future, or more complicated, like the ten-card Celtic Cross. There are some great books that explore these approaches and a lot more. Tarot cards have a wide scope for interpretation and are a good way to practice using your own intuition.

· · · Activity 12 · · ·
An Easy Daily Tarot Practice

One of the best ways to become comfortable with a tarot deck is to use it often. This doesn't mean you have to set aside a half an hour every day to do an in-depth reading. (Seriously, who has time for that?) Instead, use a notebook, or your Book of Shadows if you have one, and pull one card every day for a month. Sit with it for a few minutes and see if it resonates with anything going on in your life right now, or pull it at the beginning of the day and check in again at the end of the day to see if there is anything that makes sense with what happened in between. Write a few brief notes in whatever book you're using so you can return to it later and see if there were hints at events or experiences that occurred days or weeks or even months further on. You might be surprised! And in the meantime, you're getting better acquainted with that

Tarot Books

One of the best ways to get comfortable with the tarot is to practice with it regularly. But there are also some really helpful books for both beginners and those who are more experienced and wish to move beyond the basics. Mary Greer is one of the best known authors of books on tarot, and I highly recommend her books. Try *Tarot for Your Self: A Workbook for Personal Transformation* (2nd Edition, Weiser, 2002) and *Mary K. Greer's 21 Ways to Read a Tarot Card* (Llewellyn, 2006). Another great resource is Barbara Moore, who not only writes books about how to use tarot but has also created a number of fun decks of her own. I highly recommend *Your Tarot Your Way: Learn to Read with Any Deck* (Llewellyn, 2016), *Tarot for Beginners: A Practical Guide to Reading the Cards* (Llewellyn, 2010), and *Tarot Spreads: Layouts and Techniques to Empower Your Readings* (Llewellyn, 2012).

particular deck. If you don't feel as though you are connecting with the deck after a week or two, you might want to try switching to another.

Oracle Decks

Oracle decks tend to be simpler and easier to use than tarot and can vary in number anywhere from twenty-some to more than eighty cards, though most tend to be somewhere in the middle. Like tarot, oracle cards usually have some kind of theme and beautiful illustrations, so you can choose the one that appeals to you the most. Or have a variety to suit your changing needs and moods. (I own about a dozen. Or maybe more. I haven't counted lately.) While oracle cards can be used in spreads like tarot cards, they are generally pulled one at a time or up to three if you need clarification. Like tarot decks, oracles often (but not always) come with booklets that can help guide you in interpreting the cards. Unlike tarot cards, there is no learning curve with oracle decks, since the cards tend to be very specific and obvious. (For instance, in my *Everyday Witch Oracle*, we have cards like "Hibernation and Regeneration" and "Follow Your Dreams," and the guidebook not only gives a basic explanation of the card but also suggests an action, a magical activity, or a divination interpretation. Easy peasy.) Oracle cards still offer an opportunity to use your own intuition but it generally isn't as much of a necessity as with tarot cards.

Rune Stones

Rune stones aren't always made of stone, although they can be. I have three sets: one I made myself out of clay, one I bought, and one I was gifted by a friend who created a stunningly gorgeous set out of fused glass (my favorite). There are a few different types, but the ones most commonly used by modern witches are known as the Elder Futhark, which originated with the Norse and Germanic tribes of northern Europe. A set consists of twenty-four runes, or symbols, which represent the forces of nature and common objects (like Eihwaz the yew, Uruz the wild ox, and Kenaz the hearth fire). Most sets also contain a blank stone known as Wyrd, which stands for the unknown or sometimes "sorry, no answer now." Rune stones are usually pulled one at a time, although there are a few basic spreads using two, three, or four runes. Again, the past/present/future spread is one of the most common and easy to understand. Although the runes are based on ancient symbols, their meanings are still applicable for today's witch. For instance, if you ask if a project is going to be successful, and you get Gifu, which means gift, the answer is probably a positive outcome. Rune stones are easiest to use for simple or yes/no answers. Most sets of stones come in a drawstring bag, and you can either do readings by putting your hand into the bag and pulling out the one that seems to call to you, or spreading them all out upside down on a table and hovering your hand over them until you sense one that pulls more strongly than the rest. Of course, you can also just grab a random rune stone and see what turns up.

· · · ACTIVITY 13 · · ·
A Daily Rune Practice

When my first high priestess introduced our then-group to rune stones, she set us the task to pick one rune a day, write it down, and then see what happened that day. (Much like the tarot exercise above.) Not only was this fun and interesting, it was also a surprisingly good way to become better acquainted with the runes because there are only twenty-four of them to learn. She printed out a handy sheet with all the runes and their basic meanings (which she kindly allowed me to use in some of my books when I wrote them later), so it was easy to refer to each

Like tarot, if you are starting out learning to use rune stones, it can be helpful to have a good book to guide you. Try checking out *A Practical Guide to the Runes: Their Uses in Divination and Magick* by Lisa Peschel and *The Book of Runes* by Ralph H. Blum.

one as you pulled it. I also used the two books listed in the tip about rune books. After a couple of months, I had learned most of them by heart. I highly recommend trying this yourself if you are drawn to the runes.

Scrying

Scrying is the art of looking into a dark bowl filled with water, or a black mirror, or some other blank surface, and opening your mind to images that might appear there. Usually this is done in a darkened room lit by a single candle set next to your scrying tool, or outside under a full moon. Using a crystal ball is considered to be a form of scrying too. Some people are very good at this. Others (me included), never see much of anything. Don't be discouraged if this doesn't work for you. You can keep trying or decide to use some other form of divination. On the other hand, you may be one of those people who has a natural gift for it. You just never know.

Pendulums

A pendulum is one of the simplest forms of divination, and the easiest to use. Its one downside is that it is only really good for yes/no questions, or those with very limited possibilities (I'll explain that in a minute). At its most basic, a pendulum is some form of string or chain with a heavier dangle at the bottom, usually a crystal, but the bottom piece can be made of anything you can attach to the line that will swing back and forth. When you acquire a new pendulum, you first have to set or calibrate it so you will know how it gives the basic "yes," "no," or "maybe/uncertain" answers. Most pendulums either swing left to right or spin clockwise for yes, and swing right to left or spin counter-clockwise for no, but the way you find out how your particular tool works is simple. First, either ask it to "say yes" or ask it a question to which you know that the answer is positive (for instance, "Is my name Deborah Blake?). Note which way it moves. Then ask it to "say no" or ask it a question that you know the answer to is no (for instance, "Is my name Wonder Woman?"). This will set the pendulum for yes and no answers, and anything else is indefinite or unanswerable. It sounds simplistic, but

Years ago, I was taught how to make a fast, simple, and incredibly cheap pendulum: attach a paper clip to the bottom of a piece of string—it works just as well as the fancy ones!

it really works. If you need to find answers that are slightly more complicated, you can write a few choices on a piece of paper and see if the pendulum swings toward any one in particular. The trick with pendulums is to hold your hand perfectly still, so you know that the pendulum is moving, not you. In theory, you can use a pendulum to find things by holding it over a map, although I've never tried this one myself.

Dream Divination

Divination through purposeful dreaming is a very old tradition. Dreams as messages have been recorded in ancient Egypt, India, Babylon, and the Old Testament. If you have a dream that seems unusually clear and vivid, it is a good idea to write it down. But witches are most likely to use oneiromancy, a fancy word for asking a question and then doing some form of dream divination to get an answer. It may be as simple as writing your question on a piece of paper and putting it under your pillow, or it may involve spellwork, calling on the gods associated with sleep (Morpheus, Hypnos, and Epona are three possibilities), or just asking the gods to send you clarity and knowledge. It is common to use certain herbs or specific crystals to boost the power of your dreams. The most important thing, as with most Witchcraft, is to set your intention clearly and focus on it as you are falling asleep.

· · · ACTIVITY 14 · · ·
Dream Pillows

One of the most common approaches to dream divination is to create a dream pillow. You can either use a pre-made drawstring bag or take a piece of cloth and sew up three sides. Inside, you can place one or more herbs; mugwort is traditional, but some people find it too powerful, so it might be better to substitute lavender, chamomile, lemon balm, hops, or catnip. (If you have a cat, I'd suggest skipping that last ingredient or you won't get any sleep at all.) Some people also like to add gemstones like clear quartz or amethyst. If you want, you can write your question on a piece of paper and tuck it inside the pillow before sewing up the last side. Place it under your pillow and concentrate on your question as you fall asleep. You can do this for as many nights as necessary.

Other Forms of Divination

There are many other types of divination, if none of these appeal to you. Some people do divination using astrology or numerology (using numbers that have certain associations), or using the I Ching, a Chinese form of divination using special sticks. There are also the old classics, palm reading and tea leaf reading. (I've never been any good at either of those, but your milage may vary.) Just keep trying until you find the one that works best for you.

Chapter Nine
SPIRITUAL CONNECTION

Being a witch is an ongoing journey, a path we walk as we move through our lives. The daily practices suggested above are great fast and easy ways to practice our Craft as a part of our normal activities. But it is also important to occasionally take a moment to connect with the more spiritual aspects of being a witch. This sometimes means stopping for a minute, or five, or ten, and really focusing on nature, or the elements, or deity. It can also mean spending some time to connect with yourself—your innermost thoughts and feelings, your gifts, your own special magic. You are the center of your own practice, after all.

Connect with Nature

For many of us, Witchcraft is a nature-based spiritual path, and we find it both satisfying and comforting to tune in to nature on a regular basis. Obviously, the way you go about doing that will depend to some extent on variables like where you live, what season it is, how much time you can spare, and issues of mobility, among other things. I would love to walk on the beach every day, but sadly, I don't live anywhere near the ocean, so I have to find other ways to make my connections. But there are always plenty of options. Try doing some of these:

- Take a walk: I know, it sounds simple, but much of a daily Witchcraft practice is. If you can walk somewhere peaceful and full of growing things, like a park, that's great. But even if you can't, you can be mindful of the sun overhead, the songs of the birds, and whatever growing things there are. Be aware of the elements of air as the wind blows, water if it rains, fire in the rays of the sun, and the earth under your feet. If there are flowers, be sure to stop and smell them!

- Look out a window: If you can't go outside, you can still connect with whatever is outside your window. If the weather is nice enough, open the window and use your senses of sight, smell, and sound to be aware of the natural world outside. Even if you can't do that, you can look out the glass at whatever the weather is doing, or the moon if it happens to be overhead.

- Be aware of insects, birds, and all the other living things we share our world with. I live in the country, so it isn't unusual for me to look out the window and see an adorable bunny, chipmunks, squirrels, woodchucks, and even deer. During the summer, I make a special effort to get outside at dusk to watch the fireflies come out. They always seem like a little bit of nature magic to me.

Connect with the Elements

We talk a lot about the elements in a modern Witchcraft practice. There are the four obvious ones: earth, air, fire, and water. Many consider there to be a fifth element, spirit, which makes up the final point on a pentacle. While we often call on them during rituals, it is also good to be aware of them as you go about your daily life.

The elements are powerful forces of the natural world, and as witches we can tap into that power to protect us in sacred space, boost the energy of our magical work, and enrich our existence in general. Each element has its own associations and areas of greatest influence, and strengthening your connection to that element will make it easier for you to work with its power when you need it.

✳ Earth

This element is usually associated with the north (so you would put an earth altar on the north side of a room, for instance, and turn in that direction to speak to it), midnight, and winter. But don't worry, you don't have to stay up late to work with earth, that's just the time of day and year to which it is considered to have the strongest connection. Green and brown are the colors most commonly associated with earth for obvious reasons, but some folks also use black or gold. It rules the natural world, the physical body, money and prosperity, trees and plants, rocks and crystals, animals (both wild and domestic), and death. The earth zodiac signs are Capricorn, Taurus, and Virgo. Those who fall under these signs tend to be the most grounded but also stubborn and hard to move, which makes sense when you think about it. If you want to represent earth on an altar, or just have reminders of its presence around your home, try using crystals or even common rocks that appeal to you in some way, green or brown candles, living plants or cut flowers, and stone or clay statues. Salt is also sometimes used to represent earth in rituals.

· · · ACTIVITY 15 · · ·
Grounding and Centering

Grounding and centering can be an important part of ritual work, but it can also help you to stay calm and focused on a daily basis, or when you need it. If possible, do this outside, under a tree or on a patch of grass. This can be done sitting, lying down, or standing. If you can't sit on the ground, you can sit in a chair and make sure your feet are connecting with the land. Close your eyes and feel the ground underneath you. If you are next to a tree, lean your back against it, or if you are lying on the ground, spread out your palms against it. Take a few deep breaths and feel the power of earth. Visualize small roots coming out of your body wherever it is connecting with the land and reaching down through the surface, down deeper below the soil, growing longer and longer until they are a part of the ground. Feel the earth energy ground and energize you, and let it flow upward from your feet or tailbone until it reaches the top of your head and meets up with the energy from the sky. Bask in that feeling for as long as you want, then pull those roots back up into your-self, knowing that the connection to the earth is always there, waiting to nourish and ground you.

Air

Air is all around us, but ironically, we rarely notice it unless it is doing something dramatic, like lifting a house and blowing it out of Kansas. (Thankfully, that rarely hap-pens.) Air is associated with the direction east, dawn, and the season of spring. This element is often represented by the color yellow, although you can use pale blue, laven-der, or any other soft color you prefer. It rules commu-nication and thought, the intellect and ideas, as well as new beginnings. Air's zodiac signs are Aquarius, Libra, and Gemini, and those who fall under these signs tend to be good communicators who are led more by intellect than emotion, but they can also be changeable and unpredictable (much like the air, which can turn from a gentle breeze to a dangerous tornado). This element can be represented on your altar or in rituals by incense, a feather, or even a pen.

• • • ACTIVITY 16 • • •
Wind and Weather

Give yourself the challenge of going outside in all sorts of weather, and being aware of how the air feels. Greet the dawn when the slightest mist is still around, or let a gusting wind move your hair and clothing. Make friends with the air in all its changeable forms. If you want, you can sing a chant to it, since your voice uses air to speak or sing.

Fire

Fire is associated with the direction of south, with noon, and with summer. This makes sense, when you think of heat, since these are all the hottest places and

To connect with air quickly and easily, just breathe. Take a few minutes to concentrate on the movement of the element in and out of your lungs, becoming part of you as you inhale, being changed inside your body before you return it.

times. This element's colors are red, orange, and bright yellow/gold, all the colors of fire itself. It rules passion, energy, creativity, courage, healing, and the blood. Fire's zodiac signs are Aries, Leo, and Sagittarius. These folks tend to be bold, active, and passionate. Occasionally, they can be a little hotheaded. This element is usually represented on the altar by a candle or some other flame (if you can't have a live flame, a faux one is fine), but a red stone like carnelian or a symbol of fire or the sun will do just as well.

• • • ACTIVITY 17 • • •
All Fired Up

There is no better way to connect with fire than by standing by a roaring bonfire and watching the flames dance, smelling the smoke, and listening to the crackle of burning logs. It is one of my favorite things to do. Of course, not everyone has the space to have a bonfire (and there are many parts of the country where the risk of wildfires is too great for outdoor open flames, alas). There are a number of alternatives, and you can choose whichever one works for you best. If you can't have a bonfire, there are many free-standing fire pits that can be set up in a back yard or even a patio, depending on their size. Small propane fueled fire-pits have become very popular, and

FIRE WITHOUT FLAMES

Not everyone can have an open flame. Some folks live in places that forbid it (for example, dorm rooms) or might be traveling and staying in hotels. Some of us have animals that can't be trusted with actual fire. There are some very good faux candles available these days, some of which even mimic the flicker of a real candle. They're not as good as the actual thing, but if you want to connect with the element of fire and circumstances restrict you, they make a good substitute. If I am doing a spell I want to keep going for a long time, I will start with a real candle and when I have to leave the room or go to bed, I turn on a battery-operated version and blow out the real one. The symbolism is the same.

you can even find ones that fit on an outside table. If you can't have a fire outside, consider building yourself a faux bonfire by taking a fireproof container (a cast-iron cauldron is nice, but even a large pottery bowl will work), filling it partway with sand, and then placing a number of small tea lights inside. When they are all lit together, the flames become a mini fire-pit. Of course, you should always exercise caution when dealing with fire of any size: be careful of sparks, animals getting too close, or trailing sleeves. Make sure you have a way to extinguish your fire nearby, no matter what form of this element you are using.

Water

Water is associated with the direction of west, with twilight and with the autumn. Its colors are blue, blue-green, gray, and other shades that might be found in water itself. It rules the emotions, intuition, fertility, and cleansing. Water's zodiac signs are Cancer, Pisces, and Scorpio, and those under these signs are often emotional, intuitive, and sensitive. Sometimes they go with the flow, but they can be overwhelmed by emotions if they're not careful. Water is usually represented on the altar and in rituals by a bowl or goblet full of water, but you can also use a seashell, sea glass, or anything else that evokes a sense of the element for you.

· · · ACTIVITY 18 · · ·

Power Up Your Water

Water is an easy element to connect with because we can drink it, taking its power into us in much the same way as we connect with air by breathing. But if you want to take this to another level, you can make up a batch of Power Water. Power Water is simple to make: Take a quartz crystal and make sure it is very clean. Place it in a clear glass container with a cover. If you want, you can add a favorite fresh herb, such as rosemary (if you want to sharpen your intellect or work on protection) or mint (to draw prosperity or heal). Cover the container and hold it in front of you, visualizing the water beginning to glow with energy and vitality. Place it outside under a full moon, on a windowsill where the moonlight shines, or on your altar. Repeat the visualization every day for three days, or if you're not good at that sort of thing (not everyone is), just ask the water to become more powerful, filled with positive energy. Once it is done, you can remove the herbs and crystal. (If you included herbs, you may wish to refrigerate the Power Water if you

DANCING
IN THE RAIN

One of the easiest ways to connect with the element of water is standing outside when it's raining. You don't have to dance, but make sure you let the water touch your skin. Think about how those same drops were part of the ocean at one point, or a rainforest. Who knows how far they've traveled or what they've seen? Most of our own bodies are made up of water, so we are water and water is us. That's a pretty good reason to dance, if you ask me.

are going to drink it.) Take a sip or two every day, whenever you need a boost, or use it in your magical work.

Connect with Deity

Almost all witches believe in some kind of greater power, although the form that power takes can vary significantly from person to person. The only thing that tends to be true for most of us is that it bears very little resemblance to the traditional Judeo-Christian God most of us were raised with. (Although there are those who consider themselves to be Christian Witches or Jewish Witches, so there is an exception for everything.)

For most witches, that power is perceived as both a goddess and a god, or in the case of those who are polytheistic, multiple gods and goddesses (that's where I fall). Some follow specific deities, or have a patron/matron deity who is their primary focus. Others call on God and Goddess in a more general way, or even just "the universe" or "universal power."

As with everything else in Witchcraft, this is a very personal decision and there is no wrong way. If you are new to Witchcraft, it might take a while for you to figure out exactly how you want to connect to deity, and what names you wish to refer to it/them by. Or, as often happens,

once you open your mind and heart, a God/dess or God/
desses may show up and let you know they have chosen
you. (In which case, I advise you to pay attention!)

We invoke deity during our rituals, and usually during
simple spells as well, but there are plenty of ways to connect with God and Goddess in between formal occasions.
Here are a few suggestions.

Say Hello

Yes, it really can be as simple as that. All witches are their
own priests and priestesses; there is no need to have anyone talk to deity on your behalf. All you have to do is
speak and they will hear you. Although there is no guarantee they will answer back, of course. I usually start
each day by greeting the God and Goddess, and ask them
to send me strength and watch over me and those I love.
At the end of each day, I make sure to take a moment to
say thank you for the people and things that were important during the time in between. This is pretty informal;
I don't stand at an altar or light a candle, although you
certainly can if you like. I just talk. You can do this every
day, as I do, during times of need, or if you happen to be
sitting someplace that feels unusually sacred. Just reach
out. I assure you, they are listening.

Say a Prayer

This is usually a little more formal than just chatting with the gods, although it doesn't have to be. If we are directing a prayer at a specific deity, we often start by calling on them by name ("Great Hecate, hear my prayer"), although it is also fine to be more general ("God and Goddess, I come to you in my time of need to ask for your aid and assistance"). A prayer is usually a way to ask for help, and invoking a god or gods lets them know we are aiming our request in their direction.

Create an Altar

Some witches have an altar dedicated to a specific deity, or to both Goddess and God in a more general way. Creating an altar gives you a place to commune with deity whenever you choose, and honor them in your home. There is no right way to decorate this (or any other) type of altar. You might have a statue or statues,

To honor a specific deity, put up a picture or statue representing them. To honor some form of Goddess, look for artwork that isn't obviously Pagan but still fits your image of Her—no one needs to know!

items that are associated with that deity (such as a peacock feather for Hera, or a shell for Yemaya), candles, and so on. You can leave gifts and offerings on your altar from time to time, to show your appreciation to the deity to whom it is dedicated. Flowers, pretty stones, or food are common offerings, although different deities may have their own preferences.

· · · ACTIVITY 19 · · ·
Using Goddess Oracle Decks

There are many wonderful goddess oracle decks out that represent goddesses from around the world. One great way to connect with new goddesses and perhaps figure out which ones you feel drawn to the most, is to use a deck that has information about various goddesses. Pull a random card every day, once a week, or every full moon, and see which goddess shows up to guide you.

Do Some Research

Using goddess oracle cards is one way to learn more. But there are also many books that discuss the various deities often followed by witches and Pagans, as well as websites (although I always suggest caution when reading things online, since not everything you'll find will be accurate).

If you have witchy friends, you can also talk to them about their experiences. You never know when someone will have a connection to a god or goddess that ends up resonating with you too. If you belong to a coven or group, you can explore together, which makes it even more fun.

Channel Deity through Action

Many witches believe there is a spark of the divine in each of us and that we can manifest it through the way we walk our talk and treat others. I believe that it is possible to channel the God and Goddess by doing what I consider to be Their work—helping those who need it, protecting the environment, being kind to the people around me. I am not a god, but I can channel a little bit of deity by being a personification of what I think they wish to see in the world. What could be more magical than that?

· · · ACTIVITY 20 · · ·
Do Something Nice

Challenge yourself to do something nice every day. It doesn't have to be a big thing. Feed the birds. Say something complimentary to a stranger. Be a little more kind to those who live with you. Donate five dollars to a charity you believe in. Being nice to yourself counts, too. The point is to be mindful about channeling your inner deity in whichever way feels right to you. You might find it to be surprisingly satisfying.

Be Open

This seems simplistic but really isn't. Being open to deity means paying attention to the world around you. Do you keep seeing the same symbols or animals? Does a particular god or goddess show up repeatedly in the books you read or the shows you watch? Do they come to you in a dream, as happened to a friend of mine? Sometimes connecting with deity is as basic as sitting quietly and saying, "I am here. I am listening," and seeing if anyone answers. The gods may knock at your door, but you have to be paying attention to let them in.

Chapter 10
ABOUT SPELLS

While not all witches do spellcasting, for many of us it is a major part of our Witchcraft practice. And of course spells are a part of traditional Witchcraft, as we know from the number of people who were accused of casting them when they probably hadn't.

So what is a spell? It is a form of magic, where we use written and/or spoken words, often paired with actions and ingredients tied to that particular spell in order to bring about a specific result. All those things—the words, actions, and ingredients—help us to focus better, which gives more power to the spell. If you like, you can think of it as a prayer, but with a little more oomph.

When Spells Don't Work

Of course, not every spell works every single time. There are plenty of reasons why some spells fail. It might be that you were tired and distracted when you cast the spell and didn't have the focus you needed. If you can, try and save your spellcasting for when you have the time and space to give it the attention it needs. Sometimes spells fail because you're asking for the wrong thing or not expressing yourself clearly, like if you ask for Mr. Right and get some guy whose last name is Wright instead. (Although that actually worked out for my friend Robin.) Sometimes the answer is just "no." The gods know better than we do, and there are situations in which what you are asking for would harm or steer you down the wrong path. Or there is a lesson you need to learn from your current situation that needs to be resolved first. And sometimes you are asking for the impossible. For instance, if you cast a spell to heal someone who is dying, it may be beyond the universe's ability to grant. And let's face it, if everyone who cast a spell to win the lottery succeeded, they'd probably quit holding the lottery. If a spell doesn't work, give all of these possibilities some thought before casting it again.

Free Will and Personal Responsibility

There are two main choices available when you decide you want to cast a spell. You can either write one yourself, or if you're not comfortable doing that, you can use one that someone else has written. Either is fine, as long as you make sure that the spell suits your needs at the time, is written clearly, and doesn't interfere with free will. This last one can be a bit tricky, and not everyone agrees on it, but I do, and I'll tell you why. (It's my book, after all.)

Free will is one of the tenets of Wicca, but many witches—even those who are not Wiccan—believe in the importance of free will, especially in the context of using magic. Witchcraft is, at its core, a spiritual path based on personal responsibility. We don't say the devil made us do something; we acknowledge that we are in control of and responsible for our own actions.

That also means that we cannot take responsibility for other people's actions. Each one of us is in charge of our own lives and our own choices. If you cast a spell that impinges on that right, you are essentially stealing another person's free will. Not cool, dude. Love spells can be particularly tricky because of this. I always advise people to use extra caution when casting any kind of love spell and not to cast one *on* a specific person, but simply to trust that the gods will send you the person or persons who are right for you. Think of it this way: how would you feel if you found out that your significant other had cast a love spell on *you*? How could you trust that the love you felt for them was true and not the result of a spell? You couldn't. So keep the concept of free will in mind when you are doing magical work.

Generally speaking, I never recommend doing a spell on or for another person without asking their permission first. There are some folks (non-witches, especially) who would be very uncomfortable to discover you had done so. It wouldn't get you burned at the stake these days, but it might lose you a friend or at least their trust. As long as you limit your spellcasting to magic intended to only affect yourself, you should be fine.

Free Will

The issue of free will isn't always as obvious as the love spell example. For instance, say that someone you care for is very sick or dealing with a debilitating chronic illness. The obvious choice seems to be doing a healing spell for them ... except it isn't necessarily that simple. Some people manifest illness (usually with no conscious awareness that they are doing so) because it is something they need right at that time. Some people struggle with the challenge of ill health and it completely changes their lives, ultimately making them stronger and wiser. If you cast a healing spell on someone, you might deprive them of an important lesson or opportunity for growth. It isn't up to you to make that choice for others. Now, if someone asks you to do a spell for healing, or if you ask their permission and they grant it, then it is fine to go ahead and do the spell.

Write a Basic Spell

Even if you usually use spells written by others, it is a good idea to at least give writing your own a try. Pick a goal—something basic like prosperity, or more personal like improving family relationships—and experiment with writing something that feels right to you. It doesn't have to be long, just say what you want to say.

Whether or Not to Cast a Spell

Just because you *can* cast a spell, doesn't mean that you should. In this case, I'm not talking just about the issue of free will but also whether or not it makes practical sense to turning to spellcasting as the solution for whatever problem you happen to be dealing with at the time. Just because you're a witch and you know how to do magic doesn't mean that magic is always the best solution. This list (originally published in my 2010 book, *Everyday Witch A to Z Spellbook*, pages 3–4) will help you decide.

When *to* cast a spell:

* When you have exhausted all the mundane options but still need to achieve a goal (the spell not only puts your intention out into the universe but is also a way of asking for help)

- When the spell will affect only you (casting a spell to open yourself to love)

- When you know what you want and are willing to do the work required to get it (like putting in applications at appropriate places after asking for the perfect job)

- When only good can come from the spell

When *not* to cast a spell:

- When there is a simple solution that doesn't require magick (you need to lose five pounds, haven't tried a diet yet, and have plenty of time)

- When casting a spell would interfere with free will (casting a love spell to get a particular person, for instance)

- When you aren't sure what you really want to achieve (if you are uncertain of the end results you want, it is hard to truly focus enough will to make a spell work)

- When there is the possibility of causing harm to yourself or to others (remember, harm none)

If you're not sure whether or not casting a spell is the right way to go, you can always ask the gods/the universe or your own inner wisdom. Just make sure you pay attention to the answer. When in doubt, wait a few days and consider it again, or just deal with the problem in a more mundane way.

· · · ACTIVITY 22 · · ·
To Spell or Not to Spell

Sit down with a pen and a piece of paper and consider the issues you are dealing with in your life right now. In one column, write down the things that might be helped by casting a spell. In the other column, write the things you are pretty sure just need everyday, practical approaches.

Don't forget that even when you do magical work, it still usually requires follow-up in the form of some kind of real-world action.

Four Essentials for Spellwork

Many witches consider these four elements to be the essential tenets of spellwork. Some people call it the Witch's Pyramid. As far as I know, this is another of those Wiccan approaches that has been adopted by many witches, even those who aren't specifically Wiccan. It's something to consider, anyway.

- To Will — Have a clear idea of what you want to accomplish and the belief that your spell will work.

- To Know — Apply your knowledge as a witch and your knowledge of your own personal situation.

- To Do — Put as much energy and focus as you can into the actual spellcasting

- To Keep Silent — Once the spell is cast, don't talk about it. Follow up with concrete and constructive action in the mundane world, then let what will happen, happen.

I'll add, in the case of that last one, that you don't have to keep completely silent. There's no reason you can't tell a witchy friend or discuss it with your coven, for instance. The concept behind this tenet is that the more you talk about a spell you've cast, the more you dilute the energy you put into it, so you definitely don't want to go around bragging about it, a common newbie mistake.

Creating a Spell

Assuming you are going to write your own spell instead of using one from someone else, there are some basic steps involved. Some are optional and some are not, but if you are just starting out, it can be good to use all the tools at your disposal.

The first thing you need to do is determine your goal, or what it is you are trying to achieve with your spell. Sometimes this is obvious, but you may need to give some thought to how specific or how general you want to get. For instance, suppose you need more money, a common problem. Do you want to just ask for prosperity, or more money? Or is your situation actually that you need a better paying job with opportunities for advancement?

Here's the tricky bit: you want to be as specific as possible while still leaving the gods enough wiggle room to give you what you want in a way you may not have anticipated yourself. You'd be amazed at how often this happens. I've been making gemstone jewelry for years, and

 before most of my time got taken up by writing, I did a lot of craft shows. I used to do my favorite prosperity spell before each show. Sometimes I'd sell a lot of pieces.

Other times I hardly sold anything but met someone there who wanted to carry my jewelry in their store or invite me to take part in a later show that *did* end up making me money. Prosperity isn't always immediate and obvious. Sometimes it is more about potential, and you want to allow room in your spell for that.

· · · SPELL 2 · · ·
Deborah's Classic Prosperity Spell

This is the spell I wrote way back in the day (first published in *Circle, Coven & Grove: A Year of Magickal Practice*, Llewellyn, 2007). It has always worked very well for me.

> God and Goddess, hear my plea
> Rain prosperity down on me
> Bring in monies large and small
> To pay my bills, one and all
> Money earned and gifts for free
> As I will, so mote it be

Once you figure out your goal and more or less how you want to ask for what you need, there are a few other components of the spell you'll want to decide upon.

OPTIONAL SPELL ENDING

In a prosperity spell like this one, or some other types of spells, you may want to add an extra few words to make sure that your spell doesn't accidentally interfere with free will, or cause unintentional harm. For instance, you don't want your prosperity to come because someone you love dies and leaves you money. In these cases, I often add the following: *For the good of all, and according to the free will of all, with harm to none.* It is easy to remember and doesn't change the intent of whatever spell you are doing.

Which Gods, If Any, Will You Call On?

You may want to keep it general, and say "God and God-dess" or "Powers of the Universe." Or you may have a particular deity you consider your personal god/dess, to whom you address all your spells and prayers. Or there might be a deity who is particularly appropriate for whichever spell you're casting, such as Aphrodite or Venus for love spells, or Bast if you are trying to find the perfect familiar. Or you may choose not to call on deity at all, and simply send your spell out on its own.

Are You Going to Make Your Spell Rhyme?

Rhyming is traditional, because it is said to make the words more powerful. It also makes the spell easier to memorize (if you choose to do so) and can certainly make it sound more formal. But this is strictly a matter of choice. If you find the idea intimidating, by all means, don't worry about it. Or you can rhyme every other line. Some of my spells rhyme and some don't. It's more about the way they come to me than anything else.

Are You Planning to Read It Off a Piece of Paper or Memorize It?

Memorizing a spell allows you to say it anywhere even if the spell isn't with you, if you don't like the idea of having to hold paper or a Book of Shadows, or if you're going to be doing it when it is too dark to read. However, you may want to keep the spell short and simple. But if you are going to read it out, the length probably won't matter. I have a few spells, like the prosperity spell above, that I've used for so long that I have them memorized. Otherwise, I almost always print them out.

Handwritten versus Printed

In theory, it is more powerful to write out a spell by hand, since you are putting even more of your energy into it, and because handwriting is a very distinctive part of each individual. However, if you are like me and have terrible handwriting, or are going to be passing copies of the spell out to a group of people, it is probably more practical to print out clear copies from the computer.

Are You Going to Use Any Optional Extras?

That's what I call all the various tools and components that we add to spells to help us focus on our goal, direct our energy, or otherwise boost the power of the spell. Most witches have a stash of supplies that are used for these purposes, whether that stash is a small box hidden under the bed, assorted tools that live on their altar, or an entire cabinet dedicated to magical supplies. (In my case, it is the latter, plus a hanging cabinet on the wall above the storage cupboard that was designed as a bedside table, plus a hanging cabinet on the opposite wall filled with a large variety of gemstones. Plus the altar. What can I say—I've been doing this a long time.) Witches use correspondences to choose which items are best for which spells, such as which gemstones are associated with prosperity, or love, or healing, although as with much else in Witchcraft, not everyone agrees on these. When in doubt, listen to your gut or your inner wisdom, and chose the things that feel right to you.

· · · ACTIVITY 23 · · ·
Choosing Your Optional Extras

It's a good idea to have a list of correspondences or a few books you can use to look them up, but if you can't decide which crystal to use or which herbs would be best, try spreading them out in front of you and holding your hand over them, palm down. Move your hand slowly over your possible options, and try and see if you can get a sense of which ones are calling to you. This may manifest as a slight tingle in your palm, an itchy feeling, or even a pull toward the item. If you still can't tell, just close your eyes and reach out. Then use whatever you touch first.

Once you've figured out all the various components to your spell, sit down and write it. It might take more than one try, or it might flow out of you as if you were channeling the words of the gods themselves. (I've had it happen both ways.) Don't worry about it being perfect. As long as it says what you want it to, and you are comfortable with it, that's what matters.

Tools of the Trade

Here are some of the tools and spell components most commonly used in spellwork. Some spells are so simple, they don't need anything extra. But if you are just starting out, they can be helpful for focus and building energy to power your will before you send it out into the universe (that's why we use things that correspond with the magical work we're trying to do). You'll find many of these in the glossary at the start of the book, and there is a basic list of correspondences at the end, although you will probably end up wanting to make up your own if you use certain items often for specific purposes.

Keep in mind that if you have spells written by other people, like the ones in my books, all those optional extras are just that—optional. And it is fine to make substitutions if you don't have exactly the components you want. For instance, if a spell says to use a black candle and a piece of malachite but you don't have either, you can always use a white candle and some other green stone. Or leave out the stone altogether. If the black candle feels important, you can tie a black ribbon or string carefully around the bottom of the candle you are using instead (making sure it can't catch on fire).

Some people don't worry about candle colors (e.g., using yellow to represent the element of air) and simply use white or natural beeswax for everything. There is no wrong way.

Athame, Wand, and Staff

Although these are different tools, they are all used for essentially the same purpose: directing energy. For instance, if you are calling the quarters, you can point with any of these. If you are casting a circle and want to delineate

the boundaries as you do so, you can sketch it out in the air or on the ground with any of these tools. Some people use one, some use all, and some simply use their finger.

Chalice, Bowl, Dish

A chalice or goblet is used to hold the drink part of cakes and ale, or a libation that will be poured out to honor a deity or as an offering. It can also simply be part of the altar set-up to represent the Goddess, as well as any other type of bowl or dish. Dishes or bowls may be used to hold salt, water, herbs, or other spell components, and can be made from any material, including metal, pottery, glass, or even a large shell, although I'd stay away from anything artificial like plastic.

Cast Iron Cauldrons

In some of the more classic pictures of witches performing magic, they are seen stirring a cauldron or throwing something into one. (Don't worry, "eye of newt" is just a folk name for a kind of herb. No newts were actually harmed.) These cauldrons are almost always made out of cast iron, and are sometimes hung over a fire or seated directly on the flames. Of course, back in the Old Days, most households probably had one and it was more commonly used to make stews than spells. But a cauldron is

Representing Goddess and God During Ritual and on the Altar

It is traditional to have items on the altar representing Goddess and God. The Goddess is usually represented by an open vessel that embodies the womb, such as a cauldron, chalice, or bowl, while the God is represented by a long, thin object like an athame or wand as a symbol of the phallus. The God might also be symbolized by a deer or stag antler or a stone tower, and the Goddess by an open shell or round or oval stone that looks like an egg. Some people have statues of deity, especially if they follow specific ones. It is also fine to simply have two candles, one for each, or if the moon is full, one for the Goddess alone.

handy if you need a fire-safe container to burn something in, like a piece of paper with something you're banishing, or dried herbs. I actually have two cast iron cauldrons. One is small, sits on the table during rituals and holds my burning sage, and the other much larger one I got for ten dollars at a huge street-wide yard sale. (Seriously, it was such a find, I couldn't pass it up, but you should have seen me lugging that thing back to my car. It was HEAVY.) We sometimes fill the bottom with sand and use it to hold candles. So don't assume that you'll never be able to have one just because you can't afford a fancy new one. Check camping supply stores for smaller versions too. Keep in mind that if you are burning anything large, you will probably want to do so outside due to smoke.

Candles

Candles are one of the most commonly used tools in Witchcraft. In fact, if I am doing a simple spell, I usually just light a candle without bothering with anything else. During spellwork, candles are often used to represent the God/dess, the four quarters (traditionally east = yellow, south = red, west = blue, north = green, but you can use white for all if you prefer), and sometimes for whatever spell you are casting. For instance, you would light the quarter candles to invite in the powers of the elements/ directions, then light the God/dess candle or candles to invoke whichever deity you are working with, and then maybe a green candle for a prosperity spell or a blue candle for healing. If you are doing a spell on its own without an entire ritual to go along with it, you might just use a candle for the spell itself.

· · · ACTIVITY 24 · · ·
Candle Magic

One of the things that make candles such a handy tool is that you can do so much more with them than just burning them as is. Because they have a soft surface, you can etch symbols, runes, pentacles, your name, or your magical goal directly upon it. You can anoint them with magical oil that corresponds to your goal (being careful to avoid the wick, since oils are flammable) or roll them in crushed herbs (again,

Nothing's worse than preparing to cast a spell and realizing you're missing the one candle color you need. If you can, have the basics on hand: white (good for everything), cream, yellow, blue, green, red, black, and silver.

keeping them away from the lit end of the candle). If you don't have the color you want, you can tie a piece of colored ribbon, string, or yarn around the bottom to symbolically change the color (again—*flammable*, so use care). In addition to all this, you can burn them when you first cast the spell and then place them on an altar or some other safe surface and relight them until the candle is gone, or for a length of time, such as during the waxing or waning phase of the moon. Try taking a basic candle such as a votive or a pillar that has plenty of surface to play with, and create a candle for a magical goal. Then see how it feels to use it. Remember to focus on your goal with every step you take, because that's where the power comes from.

Stones and Crystals

There are a few stones that cover a broad spectrum of goals and are usable in many different spells. You can have a small collection and still address most magical needs with: crystal quartz, amethyst, lapis, turquoise, and garnet.

Let's face it: we witches like our crystals. It is vaguely possible that I myself have enough gemstones in various forms to outfit a small army of witches, should I ever need to do so. Like so many other aspects of spellwork, stones and crystals have certain associations with different magical goals. Luckily, many of them are good for multiple things, so you don't necessarily need to have dozens (or hundreds) in order to be set for most of the basics. Nor do you need to spend insane amounts of money, unless you want to. For example, malachite is used for prosperity work, but most green stones including inexpensive ones such as aventurine, work just as well. And you don't need to have a gigantic amethyst crystal; a small tumbled piece is just fine. As always, use what feels right to you, no matter what a book of correspondences says.

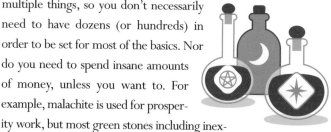

Herbs and Other Plants

Witches have used herbs throughout history and in most cultures around the world. In modern Witchcraft, we use the word fairly broadly, referring not only to actual herbs (itself a pretty comprehensive category that includes any plant with leaves, seeds, or roots that can be used for flavoring, food, medicine, or perfume) but also trees, bushes, and other plants. Herbs may be used in spells in their dried or fresh forms, or as essential oils, all of which carry the spirit or power of the plant. Incenses can be made out of herbs too, but remember that incenses made with synthetic ingredients won't work well for magic because they are missing the energetic vibrations of the real plant. As with stones, herbs have correspondences with specific magical traits and usually have more than one use.

Sage, Incense, and Purifying Herbs

All of these things are used for cleansing and clearing both ourselves and the space in which we're going to be doing ritual. When they are lit, the smoke is wafted through the air, over your body, and sometimes around the circle if you are casting one. Some people are moving away from using sage due to the issue of cultural appropriation and questions about supplies and sourcing. I'm allergic to most incense (it kicks up my asthma), and Blue Moon Circle has been using sage for the entire twenty years of our practice together (and it really works for us), so I try to make sure it is sourced ethically. There are alternative herbs, however, including lavender, cedar, sweetgrass, mugwort, rosemary, juniper, and others. Just be sparing when you use smoke inside, since you don't want to set off the smoke alarm. If you are practicing with others, make sure to check for sensitivities.

Broom or Besom

A besom is an old-fashioned style of broom traditionally made of twigs tied to a long handle. Either one can be used to sweep clean (more energetically than physically) the space where you'll be casting a spell, but they're usually only used in more formal rituals. Brooms used for magic should be used only for that.

Book of Shadows

While not every witch uses a Book of Shadows, they can be a special part of a Witchcraft practice. No two Books of Shadows are alike, since each one is the accumulated knowledge of an individual. (The only exception to this rule is a coven's Book of Shadows, which might be copied by new group members.) It is a handy place to write down all the spells you've used and whether or not they were successful. You can also use it as a place to keep the information you gather about things like herbs, stones, gods and goddesses, and anything else that is an important part of your Witchcraft practice

Once you have learned the basics of spellcasting, you can start to create your own spells or cast spells you have found that appeal to you. Spellcasting is not complicated,

Broom Bonuses

One of the great things about brooms is that almost everyone has one. If you're a witch who is still in the broom closet, no one will think anything of a pretty decorative broom hanging on your wall. They're also just a cool witchy thing to have, don't you think? And here's a fun fact: the broom is the only magical tool that represents both male and female at the same time. The female part are the bristles, and the male is the long wooden handle. Bound together, they are the perfect union of both.

but you want to make sure that you are getting it right so that the end results are positive and powerful.

How to Cast a Spell

As with every other aspect of Witchcraft, there are multiple ways to cast a spell, and the ones you choose to use will depend on your own preferences, the specific spell you're casting, and the circumstances under which you cast it. These may stay the same for every spell or change depending on a number of variables.

For example, I have known witches who never do anything more complicated than simply going outside (weather allowing) to stand under the moon or in the middle of a forest, and saying their spell out loud. If you are someone who prefers to keep things as uncomplicated as possible, this may be your style. On the other hand, there are folks who enjoy all the bells and whistles that come with a Witchcraft practice—dressing up in witchy garb, casting a formal circle, and using all the tools available to them.

For most of us, magical work falls somewhere in between. I have been working at my craft for a long time, so I don't always need to cast a circle or boost my focus. If the spell I'm doing is relatively basic, I will probably light a candle, recite the spell, and leave it at that. However, if the matter is truly important or I am working magic with my coven, I usually go through an entire formal ritual. Both approaches are equally acceptable. It just depends on what the spell is, why I'm doing it, and with whom.

If you are new to the practice of Witchcraft or are someone who has a difficult time staying focused, a more formal approach might work better for you. If you are short on time, energy, space, or privacy, a faster and more straightforward style makes more sense. It may take some experimentation to figure out what type of spellcasting fits your own particular needs and preferences. And don't be surprised if it changes over time. A Witchcraft practice will grow and shift with us if we're doing it right.

What follows are some of the generally accepted steps in spellcasting if you are doing a full ritual along with the spell. Keep in mind that you can skip any or all of these if they don't feel right to you or you don't think they're necessary for a particular spell. Or, you know, if it is Tuesday. Start by assembling all the items you'll need for the spell and the accompanying ritual. (Don't forget matches if you are lighting candles, incense, or purifying herbs. You wouldn't believe how many times Blue Moon Circle has done that.) Make sure you have privacy and that you turn off your phone. Then turn all your attention to your spell and what you wish to achieve. Note that these instructions are for an individual Witch. Working with a group is a little different, although many of the steps are the same.

Cleanse the Space You Will Be Using for Your Spellwork

You are creating sacred space, so the intention here is to get rid of anything that will interfere with your work, like lingering negativity from your daily life. You can sweep it away with a broom kept for that purpose, or walk around the perimeter of your circle with sage/incense/purifying herbs, or sprinkle water, salt, or both mixed together. Or any combination of these actions.

Cast the Circle

This act encloses you within sacred space, leaving the mundane world outside and providing you with a safe space to cast

It is traditional in magical work to move deosil (clockwise) when casting a circle, calling the quarters, and moving around the circle. Usually the only time you turn widdershins (counterclockwise) is when opening the circle or sometimes during banishing work.

your spell. You can draw a line with salt around the edges of the circle space (assuming you didn't do that in the first step), or draw an actual circle with chalk or a piece of yarn, or by turning in a circle and using an athame/wand/your finger to direct energy. I like to visualize a soft golden light springing up as I turn so that when I have come all the way around, I am enclosed in a circle of light. If you want, you can say, "The circle is cast. I am in sacred space."

If you want, you can also cleanse your own energy

This is especially important if you feel as though you are dragging unpleasant thoughts or feelings from your mundane life into your circle. Use sage or other purifying herbs to clear away confusion, anger, or anything else you don't need by wafting the smoke from head to toe and back again. Or you can mix salt and water and dab it on your third eye (the middle of your forehead), your lips, your

 heart, and your solar plexus. If you want, you can visualize that same glowing light. If you are feeling particularly scattered or filled with negative feelings, you may wish to do your personal cleansing before entering the circle. Cleansing can be energetic

only (using the purifying herbs and/or salt and water), or you can actually bathe to cleanse both your physical body and your spirit in preparation for magical work.

Call the quarters

Either turn to face each direction as you call the quarter associated with it (usually done if your circle has candles set at each quarter), or if you are lighting all the candles on an altar in front of you, just stay facing the altar. Most people start with air to the east, then fire to the south, water to the west, and earth to the north. Others start with earth. You can recite a formal invocation or quarter call, or simply say something like, "I call the power of air to join me in my circle, to protect and support me as I work my magic." Light each candle before or after you call the corresponding quarter.

Invoke the Goddess (and God, if desired)

Depending on the spell and when you are doing it, you might invoke both the Goddess and God or just the Goddess (on full moons, for instance). Remember that you can call the quarters, but when you are invoking deity, you are asking them politely to join you if they are willing. You can use formal wording, such as, "Great Goddess, I greet you and ask for your blessing on my magical work

GIFTS AND OFFERINGS

If you are going to be invoking deity, you may wish to bring some form of gift or offering into circle with you. It could be a fresh flower or flowers, incense, food, a goblet of wine, or a shiny stone. Some gods prefer specific items, and you may want to make an offering based on the deity you are working with, but it really is the thought that counts. If you are doing your spell outside, you may wish to pour out a libation of wine or juice as an offering or leave some flower petals or herbs.

done on this, your night of the full moon," or you can say something more simple, like, "God and Goddess, please join me here in sacred space and support my work." Light a candle for whichever deity or deities you invoke.

Ground and center

This basically means being as grounded and fully present in the moment as you can be. Some witches visualize sending energy down into the ground and up toward the sky, like the roots and branches of a tree. Others feel themselves settling into the space and growing slightly heavier, or lighter. Some people just take a deep breath and let it out again. (See Activity #15, Grounding and Centering, for further instructions if you're new to this.)

Optional extras

If you are using herbs, crystals, symbols, or any other extra items to help you focus your energy into the spell, now is the time to use them. You could place each item in front of a candle or on the altar, or in a dish. I like to name each thing I use out loud, for example, "Lavender for healing and love," and "Rose quartz for friendship, love, and peace," and so on. But you can simply hold the item for a moment before putting it wherever feels right to you.

Light the spell candle, if using

This can be done either before saying the spell or after, depending on the spell.

Recite the spell

This is the core of your spellcasting. Put as much focus and feeling as you can into the words as you speak them, and visualize them carrying your intent out into the universe.

Although there is a lot of power in the spoken word, silence can be surprisingly powerful too. Try doing an entire spell ritual in silence and see how it feels.

Sit with the spell

Take a few moments after saying the spell to sit in silence. If you lit one, you might want to gaze at the candle. Or you could look up toward the sky if you are outside. Let the spell settle until it feels right to come back to the mundane world.

Cakes and ale

In group work, most rituals end with cakes and ale. If you are doing a spell on your own, you may still want to have a small bite to eat and something to drink to help ground you back to reality.

Dismiss the quarters

Thank the quarters for lending their energy to your circle and let them go. Blow or snuff out their candles one by one.

Thank the Goddess and God

Thank any deities you invoked at the beginning of your spell for coming to your circle and aiding your magical work. Blow or snuff out their candles.

Open the circle

Do the reverse of whatever you did to cast the circle in the beginning, turning counterclockwise instead of clockwise. Or simply visualize the light fading away as you let the circle fall.

Chapter Eleven
SPELLS AND SPELLCASTING

The spells that follow all have suggestions for timing (days of the week, phases of the moon, time of day, etc.), along with optional supplies. Feel free to alter or ignore these suggestions if they don't fit your situation, needs, or preferences. For instance, prosperity work is often done on Thursdays. If you have a job interview on a Monday, by all means do the spell on Sunday. If a spell is most powerful when cast on the night of the full moon, that doesn't mean you can't do it some other time if you feel so inclined.

Some of the spells call on God and Goddess. If you're not comfortable with that, you can substitute something like "universal powers," leave out mention of the gods, use the name of a specific deity, or skip that part entirely.

The same applies to the spell supplies. What you'll see are items I think would be helpful, the kinds of things I might use if I were doing the spell. If you have other tools you'd rather use, absolutely do that. If you don't happen to have something, either do without it or substitute something else. Or say the spell without any accompaniments, if that's what works best for you. These are your spells, it is your Witchcraft practice, and there is no one right way.

Note that most of these spells are written to be said for yourself. If you are saying one on behalf of someone else (with their permission, of course), you may need to change some of the pronouns from I/me/myself to he/she/they or his/hers/theirs.

Almost every spell is more powerful if performed on the night of the full moon. One exception (among a few) is banishing, which is more suited for other times of the lunar cycle.

Spells

Note: The optional supplies listed are in addition to the regular ritual supplies if you are doing a full circle casting (listed earlier in this section). Even if you are not doing a full formal ritual, you may still want sage or other purifying herbs to cleanse yourself and the space you're using before you start, and a candle or candles for God/dess.

Love and Relationship Spells

These spell can help you address various love and relationship issues in ways that don't impinge on other people's free will. Still, exercise caution when doing spells that involve others.

· · · SPELL 3 · · ·
Finding Love

TIMING: Friday

SUPPLIES: Pink or red candle (pink is for romantic love, and red is for passionate love). A fresh rose or dried rose petals and/or lavender, an amethyst or rose quartz crystal or any heart-shaped stone. An empty bowl (the bowl should be pretty).

INSTRUCTIONS: Place the bowl in front of you on your altar or a table, with the other supplies next to it. As you speak the spell, place the herbs and stone inside the bowl. Light the candle last.

God and Goddess

You are blessed with the love you hold

Each for the other, consorts and partners

Love wide as the universe

And bright as the moon and stars

I am complete on my own

But the bowl of my heart is empty

And so I ask of you this boon

That you help me to find the one who will fill that emptiness

With kindness and compassion (add herbs)

With an open and loving heart (add stone)

Bringing light to my world (light candle)

As you bring light to the day and to the night

And to my spirit.

In accordance with free will and for the good of all

I ask for love

So mote it be

AFTER: Sit for as long as you want and then blow out the candle. If you have an altar or another safe place to put the bowl, leave the herbs and stone inside it. If you want, you can relight the candle (with or without saying the spell again) for as long as it lasts.

··· SPELL 4 ···

Mending a Relationship

TIMING: Dusk or before you go to bed (so that you start a new day in a better place)

SUPPLIES: A pink, light blue, lavender or white pillar or votive candle. Lavender flowers or essential oil. Rose quartz, garnet, amethyst or turquoise stone. Small bowl filled with water and a towel. Two pieces of yarn or ribbon (any of the colors listed above for the candle, or whatever you have on hand, thread will work if necessary). If you want, you can also use a picture of the person with whom you have an issue, especially if you can find one of the two of you in happier days.

INSTRUCTIONS: This spell can be used to help mend any relationship important to you, be it with a significant other, family member, or friend. While you cannot control the choices others make, sometimes just opening yourself to the possibility of healing the relationship will change the energy enough to make it possible. Make sure you are willing to follow through if the spell works. Place the herbs and stone in front of the candle. If using essential oil, dab a drop on the candle, avoiding the wick. As you are doing the spell, visualize the person you are talking about.

Note: This spell uses knot magic, a traditional form of spellwork. Knots are usually done in multiples of the magical number three. I like to use nine, but you can do three or six or however many feels right to you. (For instance, if you have known the person for seven years, you could use that number.)

It is my wish to mend this rift

To heal the hole between us

Love and friendship are a gift

Connection, talk, and trust

I wash away the hurt gone by (dip hands in water, dry)

Open now to future clear

Mending hearts for one more try

I close the gap to bring us near

(Wrap the yarn around the bottom of the candle and tie the ends together, knotting them nine times. Then light the candle.)

AFTER: If you want, visualize possible situations in which you and the other person are sitting and talking, or whatever it is you want to have happen. Blow or snuff out the candle when you're done.

· · · SPELL 5 · · ·
Full Moon Opening to Love

TIMING: Full moon (or the two nights before or after)

SUPPLIES: A white candle in a fire-safe container (that will stay cool enough to hold)

INSTRUCTIONS: There are times when we feel the need for someone else in our lives, whether it is a lover, a friend, or even the perfect animal companion. Sometimes we are lonely but aren't even sure what it is we're missing. This simple spell is perfect for those times, since all it does is open your heart to whatever it is you need. If possible, stand outside under the full moon. If you can't do that, simply stand in a quiet, dark inside space and feel the moon's energy beaming down on you. Light the candle and hold it out in front of you when you say the spell.

Blessed Lady of the moon
Shine your light on me
And help me to let my light shine out
Into the night, into the world
Opening me to love
In the best way possible
So mote it be

Prosperity and Abundance Spells

Prosperity and abundance mean different things to different people at different times of their lives, but here are a few possible approaches to fulfilling your own needs. Remember to keep an open mind and allow the universe room to provide answers you might not have thought of.

· · · SPELL 6 · · ·
Prosperity Spell

TIMING: New moon until full moon (waxing lunar cycle) or a Thursday

SUPPLIES: Green pillar or votive candle. A sharp object (athame, toothpick, anything you can use to etch the candle). Dried basil, dill, and/or mint. Any small green stone, such as malachite, aventurine, green agate, or jade. A coin (I have a fun half dollar I like to use for my prosperity magic, but anything special from a dollar coin to a very shiny quarter or penny will do). A piece of paper and a pen.

INSTRUCTIONS: When you have set up all your supplies on an altar or table and cast a circle (if doing so), take a minute to think about what kind of prosperity you need and the forms you might want it to take: for instance, say you have a lot of bills to pay and want money from an unexpected windfall—remembering to make sure that any source is positive—or you want a better job, a raise, or better control over your spending. Prosperity means different things to different people, and that meaning can change due to circumstances. Etch any symbols you want (a dollar sign, your initials or name, rune signs associated with prosperity) into the candle as you think. Write your thoughts down on the piece of paper, then put the candle in the center of the paper and the herbs and stone next to the candle. Light the candle and hold the coin in your hand as you say the spell.

God and Goddess, Powers of the Universe
I ask that you send me prosperity in all its positive forms
To fulfill my wishes and meet my needs
Building on my hard work and true desires
So mote it be

AFTER: Carefully pick up the candle and drop a few drips of wax on the middle of the paper where it was sitting. Place the coin there so it sticks to the wax. Fold the paper around the coin, herbs, and stone to make a small envelope and then seal it shut with a few more drops of wax. Blow or snuff out the candle, sending thoughts of gratitude out to the universe for whatever is to come. You can place your bundle on an altar, in your purse or wallet if it fits, under your pillow or in a drawer. If you want, you can relight the candle every night for the rest of the waxing moon and add another drop or two to your bundle. Or simply take the bundle out and hold it, sending your wish for prosperity back out again.

••• SPELL 7 •••
Reducing Debt

TIMING: At the beginning of the waning moon (right after the full moon)

SUPPLIES: Green candle, piece of paper and a pen, fire-safe container such as a small cast-iron cauldron, or a bonfire if you can be outside.

INSTRUCTIONS: This is a simple spell aimed at reducing debt, which can be a source of stress. Keep in mind that all magical work is done with the expectation that you will continue to do your part in the mundane world; this is simply to give things an extra nudge and maybe a bit of luck. You can either write the word DEBT on the paper or specific debts you want to get rid of. Then light the candle and say the spell, holding the piece of paper in your hand.

With the waning of the moon
So may my debt grow smaller
Less of a burden with every day
Leaving me freer and lighter
For the good of all and according to the free will of all
So mote it be

AFTER: Either burn the piece of paper, or if it isn't safe to do that, rip it into tiny pieces and throw it away. Blow out the candle. If you want, you can repeat this every night of the waning moon. Remember to take practical actions to reduce your debt as well.

· · · SPELL 8 · · ·
Abundance

TIMING: Full moon (or the days surrounding it)

SUPPLIES: A number of small candles (such as tea lights) set on a fire-safe plate.

INSTRUCTIONS: Abundance isn't necessarily the same things as prosperity, although there is some overlap. Abundance means having lots of positive things, whether they are physical items (like food, money, or an overflowing garden) or less tangible items (like friends, or plenty of work that you like, or love). When you do this spell, picture the ways you would like abundance to manifest in your life. Plenty of good food on the table, or enough money to have fun with, or whatever it means to you. Say the spell. Then, as you light each candle, picture or say out loud one way in which you would like to manifest abundance in your life.

Lady of the Moon

Round and full

Mother to us all

Grant me abundance

(Light the candles, saying all the ways you wish for abundance, then repeat the spell a second time.)

Protection, Grounding, and Cleansing Spells

These are all basic, yet vital, components of both a Witch-craft practice and daily survival. These spells are simple enough to do often, and whenever needed.

· · · SPELL 9 · · ·
Protection

TIMING: Dark or new moon

SUPPLIES: Black or white candle. Hand mirror or piece of black cloth. Dried rosemary. Coarse salt (sea salt or Kosher are best, but table salt is fine if that's all you have). Piece of black onyx, black tourmaline, or red jasper. Small bowl. Sage wand, purifying herbs, or any protective incense.

INSTRUCTIONS: Waft your incense or purifying herbs over all the rest of your supplies. Sprinkle a little of the salt in a circle around you and around the candle. Pick up the rosemary and say, "Rosemary, for pro-tection." Do the same with whichever stone you're using. Light the candle, and as you say the spell, aim the mirror out away from you (or hold up the black cloth) and visualize it reflecting back anything nega-tive or harmful back out into the universe.

Protected am I

By stone and herb

By light and land

By faith and magic

Protected am I

From all that would harm

From all that would hurt

From all sent in darkness

Protected am I

Protected am I

Protected am I

From this moment forward

So mote it be

AFTER: If you want, you can carry the stone with you, especially if you are feeling threatened or anxious. You can also close your eyes and visualize that mirror reflecting anything negative or malicious away from you, back to where it came.

· · · Spell 10 · · ·
Calm and Grounding

Timing: Any

Supplies: White candle in a firesafe container. Small bowl of lavender. Bowl with water plus a towel. Rose quartz crystal. Small drawstring bag. Calming background music or ocean sounds. Sage/purifying herbs.

Instructions: Turn on quiet music if desired. Waft sage or purifying herbs from head to toe, then cleanse your hands with water to wash away the cares and stresses of the world. Dry your hands on the towel. Smell the lavender and breathe deeply, running your fingers through the herb if you want, then put some into the drawstring bag. Hold the crystal in your hands and feel its calming energy. Hold it to your chakra points (top of head, third eye in middle of forehead, throat, heart, solar plexus, navel, and base) and feel it pulling out all the frantic energy we all normally carry with us. Put the crystal in the bag with the lavender and close it. Light the candle and say the spell while holding the bag in your hand or lap.

I wash away my cares and worry

No more rushing, no more hurry

With these herbs and with this stone

I soak up calm down to the bone

Grounded now and breathing deep

This sense of peace I still will keep

Even in the midst of strife

Calm and grounded for my life

So mote it be

AFTER: Sit quietly for as long as it feels right and enjoy the feeling of being calm and grounded. Whenever things get too crazy in your life (or once a day, if you want to add it to your routine), sit with the bag in your hands and remind yourself to let go of the stresses of the day.

· · · SPELL 11 · · ·

Cleansing Body and Spirit

TIMING: Full moon

SUPPLIES: Sea salt (regular salt will do if necessary). Lavender flowers or essential oil and chopped lemon peel or essential oil. Quartz crystal. Jar with a lid. Water.

INSTRUCTIONS: A few hours or a day before you are going to do this spell, place the salt, herbs (or a few drops of each essential oil) and the crystal into the jar. Shake it gently three times, then put it somewhere safe, like your altar if you have one. If you can, leave it where the moonlight can hit it. When you are ready to do the spell, pour a little of the water into a container you can take into the shower or bath with you. As you bathe, anoint yourself with the water or pour it over yourself. Then say the brief spell.

Note: If you are allergic to either lavender or lemon, you can do without the herb or substitute a different herb with cleansing or purifying qualities.

With the power of the moon and the Goddess
I am cleansed, body and spirit

AFTER: You can keep the remaining water and use it until it is gone. If you are going to keep it for a while, you might want to refrigerate it.

Growth and Success

Success comes in many different forms, and growth in necessary for forward movement in your life. Try these spells and see which ones resonate with you the most.

• • • SPELL 12 • • •
Personal Growth

TIMING: New moon through full moon (waxing phase)

SUPPLIES: Green candle. Small pot full of soil. Herb or flower seeds. Book of Shadows (if you have one) or any blank book or notebook plus something to write with. Small pitcher of water.

INSTRUCTIONS: This is a good spell to do when you are ready to commit to personal growth in whatever way works for you at the time. Part of Witchcraft, I believe, is continuing to learn and grow, both as a human being and as a witch. Place all your supplies on an altar or table. Think about the ways in which you would like to grow and progress. The book is the symbol of future learning, and the seeds are the symbol of growth. Push the seeds into the soil and pour some water onto

them, then place the pot by the book or notebook, light the candle, and say the spell.

> Seeds are planted, soil is watered
>
> Goddess shine your light on me
>
> As the moon grows ever larger
>
> Send me growth and clarity
>
> Learning, reaching, stretching out
>
> Being all that I can be
>
> Like the seeds that I have planted
>
> Let me grow like a strong tree

AFTER: If you have goals or plans, you can write
them in your book or notebook. Do your best to
nurture the seeds you planted.

· · · SPELL 13 · · ·

Achieving Goals and Success

TIMING: Anytime during the waxing moon or full
moon, Lammas or Mabon, or a Sunday

SUPPLIES: White candle. Piece of paper and a pen.
A sharp instrument to etch the candle (athame,
toothpick). If you want, you can use a picture that
symbolizes your goal.

INSTRUCTIONS: Etch words or symbols that represent your goals (or what you wish to succeed at) into the side of your candle. Light it and recite the spell.

Note: If you are saying this at one of the sabbats, say "God and Goddess" instead of Goddess.

Goddess, grant me success

Let me have the strength and energy

To work toward my goals

The good fortune to find all that I need

To help me along the way

And the generosity to share whatever I achieve

With those who still strive

Goddess, grant me success

In all my endeavors

AFTER: You can repeat this as often as needed, especially if it helps remind you to do whatever it takes to work toward your goals.

Healing

We all need healing from time to time, whether it is physical, emotional, psychological, or psychic. Remember to be kind to yourself and give yourself space to heal when necessary. You're worth it.

· · · SPELL 14 · · ·
Healing the Body

TIMING: Waxing moon (new moon to full moon), full moon, or a Monday

SUPPLIES: Large blue candle. Healing herbs such as calendula, lemon balm, lavender, or mint. A picture of yourself (or if you are doing this on behalf of someone else—with their permission—or for a pet, use a picture of them). Alternatively, you can make and use a poppet instead of a picture.

INSTRUCTIONS: Place the picture (or poppet, if using) on your altar or table and put the candle behind it in a fire-safe holder. Sprinkle the herbs over the picture or poppet, and light the candle.

Note: If saying the spell for someone other than yourself, you will have to change a few words, such as "I call upon *their hidden strength*" instead of "*my own.*"

I call upon the powers of the elements

Earth, Air, Fire, and Water

I call upon the powers of the universe

Goddess and God

I call upon my own hidden strength

Deep in the cells of my body

And invite in healing

Welcome in healing

Encourage healing

Increasing my healing with every passing day

Healing is mine

So mote it be

• • • ACTIVITY 25 • • •
Making a Poppet

Poppets are small crude dolls that are created to represent a person. They are symbolic, so that the magical work done on the poppet will transfer to the person the doll represents. (This is intended to be used in a positive way.) To make a poppet, fold a rectangular piece of cloth in half, draw a basic human figure onto it and

cut it out, leaving it attached at the fold at the top of the head. Using a needle and thread, sew the poppet together around the edges, leaving a space through which you can stuff it with cotton balls, tissue, or whatever you intend to use as stuffing. If a poppet is being used for a specific magical purpose, you can add dried herbs that would suit that task. Then finish sewing it up. You can draw a face, or sew on yarn for hair, or anything else that will make the poppet look at least vaguely like the person it is supposed to represent. The poppet is now ready for use.

· · · SPELL 15 · · ·
Healing the Spirit

TIMING: Dark moon, or dark moon through full moon

SUPPLIES: White or light blue candle. Sage, incense, or purifying herbs. Dried or fresh lavender and rosemary in two small bowls. Bell or chime.

INSTRUCTIONS: Make sure you perform this spell in a quiet, dim space. Light the candle and gaze at it for a while, then waft the smoke from the sage/ incense/purifying herbs over your body, concen-

trating especially on your head and heart. Run
your fingers through the lavender and rosemary
and then over your body, so the scent clings to you.
Ring the bell or chime (if using), and return your
focus to the candle as you say the spell.

Like the light of this candle

My spirit grows brighter (ring bell)

Like these healing herbs

My spirit grows strong (ring bell)

Like this sacred smoke

My spirit is purified (ring bell)

My mind is healed (ring bell)

My heart is healed (ring bell)

My spirit is healed (ring bell)

As I say, so must it be

AFTER: Continue to gaze at the candle as long as feels
comfortable, feeling the healing magic settle
into you. Relight the candle as needed,
with or without saying the spell.

· · · SPELL 16 · · ·
Letting Go

TIMING: Dark moon or Samhain

SUPPLIES: A small black candle in a holder (a tiny chime candle, birthday candle, or tea light—something small enough that you can watch it burn down until gone or almost gone). If you can't find black, white is fine.

INSTRUCTIONS: Light the candle and let it burn down for as long as you can. As it is burning, focus on all the things about yourself or your life that are holding you back, and imagine them disappearing with the candle wax. Change the wording of the spell to suit your own specific needs, and/or leave out whatever doesn't apply to you.

I let go of negative attitudes

I let go of bad habits

I let go of self-sabotage

I let go of people who don't have my best interests at heart

I let go of relationships that harm me

I let go of wasted time and energy

I let go of unwise choices

I let go of anything and everything that stands in the way

Of my living my best life

So mote it be

AFTER: If you have a hard time letting go of things, you may want to stock up on small candles and do this often.

Divination and Psychic Ability

Everyone has a touch of psychic ability, but it may take a little practice to feel comfortable with it. Try using these spells to help you flex your divination muscles.

· · · SPELL 17 · · ·

Divination

TIMING: Full moon or any time you are doing divination work for yourself or others (summer solstice and Samhain are good sabbats for it)

Like any other ability, psychic ability grows stronger the more you use it. Think of it as a muscle: if you use it often, it will almost always grow stronger with time.

Supplies: Divination tools (tarot or oracle deck, rune stones, pendulum, etc.). Purple or white candle. Clear quartz crystal.

Instructions: Do this spell before divination work. Light the candle and place the crystal on top of whatever tool you are using, then say the spell.

> May my sight be clear and true
> As I do this divination
> May my hands be steady and my wisdom be guided
> By the powers that watch over us all

· · · Spell 18 · · ·
Increasing Psychic Ability

Timing: Full moon or Monday

Supplies: Purple (or white) candle. Stick of cinnamon. Cup of hot water or tea. Divination tools, if you use them.

Instructions: Everyone has some psychic ability, although not everyone has an obvious gift. This spell is to help you tap into that potential. Light the candle. Dip the stick of cinnamon into the hot water/tea and stir clockwise nine times. Set cinna-

CONNECTING WITH GODDESS

You don't need to wait for the full moon to commune with the Goddess. Nor do you need to cast a spell or be in sacred space. She is everywhere, always. I talk to the gods first thing in the morning when I wake up, asking them to help me with my day. I say goodnight to them last thing at night, and thank them for whatever came my way. Sometimes I just talk to the Goddess because I am moved to do so. I know that she is always listening, even if there is not an obvious reply. Try it, if you don't already.

mon aside. Hold the amethyst over the steam and then put it against your third eye in the middle of your forehead. (Make sure the stone isn't too hot.) Put it back down and take three sips of the tea, then say the spell.

I open myself to vision clear

Seeing things both far and near

Past and present, future too

Psychic talents old and new

Grow and flourish like a flower

While I safely use my power

AFTER: If you want, use one of your divination tools and see how it feels.

Connecting with Deity and Nature

Connection with the gods and nature are at the core of a Witchcraft practice. Try these spells to deepen that connection.

· · · SPELL 19 · · ·

Connecting with Goddess

TIMING: Full moon

SUPPLIES: White or silver candle in a firesafe holder. If you are trying to connect with a particular Goddess, you may want a symbol that represents Her, such as an owl for Athena or a cat statue for Bast. But really, all you need is your heart and spirit.

INSTRUCTIONS: Do this outside under the moon if possible. (If not, simply visualize the full moon. It is still up there, after all, even if you can't see it.) Sit or stand comfortably. Light the candle and hold it up to the sky.

Goddess, I come before you

On this, your night of the full moon

And offer myself up

For your wisdom and guidance

Goddess, hear me

Goddess, see me

Goddess, be with me

Now and forever

AFTER: Once you have said the spell, simply stand in silence and see if you can feel Her presence. You might even get a message, you never know.

• • • SPELL 20 • • •

Connecting with Nature and the Elements

TIMING: Daytime

SUPPLIES: Cup of water (rainwater, if you have a chance to collect some, or snowmelt if it is winter, or ocean/river water if you live near one). Red candle (or a small bonfire, if you can be outside and have a safe place to light one). Sage or incense or purifying herbs in a holder or fire-safe container. A small potted plant.

INSTRUCTIONS: If you can be outside for this spell, that makes it even more powerful, but even inside we are surrounded by the elements. Open a window if you can't be outside (unless it is too cold). Take a moment to feel the sun on your face if that is possible. Notice the way the air feels. Is there a breeze? Does it carry a scent with it? If it is raining, listen to the sound and put a hand into it if you like. If not, dip your fingers into the cup of water. If you are having a bonfire, light it and listen to the crackling noise and smell the smoke. If not, light your incense, sage, or herbs and watch the way the smoke moves in the air like a living thing. Light your candle if using. Say the spell, then spend a few more minutes really paying attention to the elements and the natural world around you.

Water, bringer of life

I am made up of you, and I am grateful

Air, invisible yet powerful

You let me breathe, and I am grateful

Fire, warmth and cooking

You are so useful, and I am grateful

Earth, from which we all spring

And to which we return, I am so grateful

Thank you for your gifts

I am so grateful

AFTER: Try to pay extra attention to the elements in the world you both share.

Surviving and Thriving

There is more to life than just surviving, although that's a good place to start. These spells should help to get through life's difficult times and rise above to make the most of your situation.

··· SPELL 21 ···

Increase Energy

TIMING: Full moon, waxing moon, summer solstice

SUPPLIES: Red or orange candle. A piece of garnet, jasper, malachite, or tiger's eye. A chunk of lemon, lime, or orange (or all three). A glass or goblet of water.

INSTRUCTIONS: Most of us could use more energy most of the time. (I know I could.) This is a simple spell you can do as often as you need it, although the times listed above might be the most powerful. Light the candle. Hold on to your stone for a minute or two and feel the potential for energy within it. If you can, feel that energy resonate inside you (probably around your solar plexus, but you might feel it somewhere else). Squeeze the citrus juice into the water and place the glass or goblet in front of the candle with the stone sitting next to it.

I am one with the earth, and draw energy from its power

The sun feeds my body and the moon feeds my spirit

And together, they lend me their power

The fruits the sun nourishes glow with life and vitality

I take that energy inside me and make it my own

So I too glow with energy

So mote it be

AFTER: Drink the infused water slowly, savoring every sip. If you want to save some for later, put it in a jar in your refrigerator and take a few sips whenever you feel the need.

··· SPELL 22 ···
Depression Banishing

TIMING: Waxing moon or dark moon, or a Saturday.

SUPPLIES: Black candle (white is fine if you don't have a black one). Black ribbon or yarn. St. John's Wort, basil, bergamot, geranium, or lavender either in herb or incense form. Piece of black onyx or moonstone or rose quartz or turquoise. Sage, incense (if you are using the herb in incense form), or purifying herbs.

INSTRUCTIONS: Depression can be a serious issue and not one you should rely on magic alone to deal with if you are having a really tough time. That said, a little magical assistance never hurts, and this spell may help you banish some of the blues. Place the stone and herbs (if using) in front of the candle. Light the sage or incense or purifying herbs and waft them over yourself starting at your feet. Visualize the smoke chasing the depression out of your body until it leaves out the top of your head. Light the candle and pick up your piece of ribbon or yarn. As you recite the spell, slowly tie nine knots in it.

With the power of one, my depression I bind
With the power of two, my depression I banish
With the power of three, I clear my own mind
With the power of four, my depression will vanish
With the power of five, the light grows much brighter
With the power of six, I let go of grieving
With the power of seven, my spirit is lighter
With the power of eight, I feel sadness leaving
With the power of nine, so do I will it
This I have said, and so I'll fulfill it

THE POWER OF
THE POSITIVE

Remember that in addition to medication and professional help, a positive attitude can really make a difference. One of the tough parts of depression is how easily one can become lost in negative thoughts that can overwhelm to the point where it is difficult for anything light to get in. Practice rephrasing negative thoughts with positive ones. "I'm worthless" becomes "Hey, I'm trying my hardest. Plus I took out the garbage." After all, just like magic, this is about will and focus. If you need an extra reminder, bless and consecrate a crystal for positive magical energy to carry in your pocket. When you have a negative thought, take a second to touch the crystal and let it help you turn that thought around.

AFTER: You can either put your knotted cord on your altar as a reminder, or put it someplace safe. In a month or two, or when it feels right, you can bury or burn it.

· · · SPELL 23 · · ·
Dreams Come True

TIMING: Full moon, blue moon, Lammas, Mabon, or any time that feels right to you

SUPPLIES: White candle. A bowl with salt and a bowl with water. Sage, incense, or purifying herbs. Drawstring bag or square piece of fabric (about 4 by 4 inches) plus a needle and thread. Lavender flowers, chamomile, rose petals (you can use all three or as many as you have). A piece of amethyst, aventurine, or malachite. Small piece of paper and a pen. Additionally, you can use something that represents whatever you're dreaming of, such as a coin for a money-related issue, a heart for a love-related issue, or anything else that symbolizes your ambition. If you really want to go that extra step, you can add an item to represent you, like a small lock of hair, a fingernail clipping, or a drop of blood on a tissue.

INSTRUCTIONS: This is a powerful spell to help bring an important dream to fruition. Don't use this for the little stuff; this one is for whatever dream really matters to you, no matter how impossible it seems. You are going to be creating a dream bag. You can either use a premade drawstring bag or fold over your square of cloth and sew three sides shut to make a bag of your own. Place your herbs and stone inside. Write your dream or goal on the piece of paper and place that inside along with anything else you're using. Either pull the bag closed or sew up the last side so it is complete. With each step, keep your dream firmly in mind. The last step is to bless and consecrate your dream bag. Sprinkle it with water and say, "With the power of water, I bless and consecrate my dreams." Sprinkle it with salt and say, "With the power of earth, I bless and consecrate my dreams. Light your sage or incense or herbs and say, "With the power of air, I bless and consecrate my dreams." Light the candle and say, "With the

power of fire, I bless and consecrate my dreams."
Hold the dream bag firmly in your dominant hand
and recite the spell with as much focus and will
and energy as you can muster.

Dreams can come true

This I believe

With all my heart and spirit

My dreams will come true

This I believe

With all my heart and spirit

So mote it be

AFTER: Place the dream bag under your pillow.
Repeat the spell every night before bed (without
any of the accompanying actions or supplies).

· · · SPELL 24 · · ·

Patience

TIMING: New moon might be a particularly good
energy for this, but it can be done whenever it
is needed

SUPPLIES: White candle.

INSTRUCTIONS: It can be hard to wait for the things that we want ... or, you know, dinner. But most things in life can't be rushed. This is a simple spell to help us during those times when we are feeling particularly impatient or having a hard time waiting for specific events or outcomes. Light the candle. Then wait. Then wait a little longer. When it feels right to you, say the spell and then watch the candle burn down for a while in silence.

The clock ticks
The hours go by
The moon above
Moves through the sky
Patience comes
Like grains of sand
Slowly trickling
Through my hands
I will learn
To wait with grace
Until all things
Fall into place

... SPELL 25 ...
Confidence

TIMING: Full moon, summer solstice, Sundays

SUPPLIES: Orange or red candle. Piece of carnelian, agate, amethyst, or lapis. Ginger tea, or a piece of ginger candy. (If you don't have ginger tea, you can take a slice of cut root and let it sit in hot water and it will be the same thing.) Sage or purifying herbs.

INSTRUCTIONS: When you need an extra boost of confidence in general, or before an important event, try this spell. Light the candle. Hold the stone in your hands for a while and feel its energy seeping into you. Drink a little of the ginger tea or eat the ginger candy and feel the herb's heat firing you up. Then say the spell.

I am strong and I am brave

I can do the tasks set before me

I put my best foot forward

And others see me in the best light

I am confident

And I will succeed at whatever I attempt

So mote it be

AFTER: If you want, carry the stone as a reminder to feel as strong and confident as you did when you said the spell.

· · · SPELL 26 · · ·
Travel Protection

TIMING: As needed, usually a day or two before you are going to be traveling

SUPPLIES: Black candle. Small piece of black onyx or red jasper. A sprig of fresh rosemary (dried is okay). Small drawstring bag.

INSTRUCTIONS: Traveling these days is full of hazards and many things that can go wrong. To keep disruptions to a minimum, do this spell before you travel. This is also a spell you can do for someone else (as long as you have their permission) if they will be on the road or in the sky. Place the stone and the rosemary into the bag. Light the candle and hold the bag while saying the spell.

God and Goddess

Keep me safe on my travels

Guard me from harm

Whether intentional or accidental

Let my travel go smoothly

And without incident

And let me return home safely

To find all as it should be

God and goddess

Keep me safe on my travels

So mote it be

AFTER: Carry the bag tucked into a pocket or someplace else close. (If you want, you can even make a separate one for your luggage!)

CONCLUSION

You have come to the end of the book, but you are only just beginning the first steps on the journey of whatever comes after that. Whether you are a long-time witch or just playing around with the idea to see if it fits, I hope that the contents have been helpful and useful. Of course, as the author of numerous books on Witchcraft, I always hope that.

But I also hope you had fun along the way. That you learned something that maybe you hadn't known, or discovered a different way to look at something you had. I hope that something between these pages inspired you, moved you, made you say "Aha!" or even laugh. I love to make people laugh.

Witchcraft is a very personal religion and a truly individual spiritual path. Unlike most established religions where there is a right and wrong way to do things along with general parameters most people observe, Witchcraft is kind of a "do it yourself, make it up as you go along, figure it out over time" kind of path. And you know what? I think that's a good thing.

We are, after all, each made up of all our experiences, our hopes and dreams, our successes and our failures. It makes sense to me that since we are all different, our vision of Witchcraft will also differ between us. There will be many things we agree on and some we don't, although I do believe that we have more in common than what separates us, no matter how it might sometimes seem.

Witchcraft is a never-ending journey of learning, growth, and change as we all strive to become the best witches and the best human beings that we can be. I hope that this book has helped you to take a few more steps along that journey, and I wish you well on all those that lie ahead.

Blessed be,

Deborah
Blake

CORRESPONDENCES

Correspondences are magical associations useful for putting together spells and rituals, as well as decorating an altar set aside for a particular purpose. This is a very basic list; there are entire books dedicated to this topic alone if you want to delve further.

Prosperity/Abundance
GODS/GODDESSES: Ceres, Demeter, Fortuna, Freya, Proserpina, Saturn, The Dagda

STONES: Aventurine, bloodstone, citrine, jade, malachite, tiger's eye, turquoise

HERBS: Basil, cinnamon, clove, dill, ginger, patchouli, peppermint, sandalwood

COLOR: Green

RUNE SYMBOLS: Fehu, Daeg, Othel, Gifu, Uraz, Tir

Protection

GODS/GODDESSES: Bastet, Bes, Heimdall, Isis, Sekhmet, Thor

STONES: Agate, amber, amethyst, black onyx, carnelian, citrine, crystal quartz, garnet, jade, jet, lapis, malachite, moonstone, red jasper, turquoise

HERBS: Basil, chamomile, cinnamon, dill, eucalyptus, garlic, geranium, juniper, parsley, rose, rosemary, sage

COLORS: Black, white

RUNE SYMBOLS: Thurisaz, Eihwaz, Eolh, Kenaz

Healing/Peace

GODS/GODDESSES: Apollo, Belenus, Brigit, Eir, Isis, Kuan Yin, Morpheus, Nuada, Rhiannon

STONES: Amber, amethyst, aventurine, bloodstone, carnelian, crystal quartz, fluorite, garnet, hematite, jade, jasper, jet, lapis, malachite, onyx, smoky quartz, sodalite, turquoise

HERBS: Apple, calendula, catnip, chamomile, dill, eucalyptus, geranium, lavender, lemon balm, peppermint, rose, rosemary, thyme

COLORS: Blue, black (to banish illness), green (growth)

RUNE SYMBOLS: Uraz, Kenaz, Sigel, Tir, Ing

Love

GODS/GODDESSES: Aengus, Aphrodite, Astarte, Bastet, Cupid, Eros, Freya, Hathor, Inanna, Ishtar, Isis

STONES: Agate, amethyst, garnet, jade, lapis, malachite, moonstone, rose quartz, turquoise

HERBS: Apple, basil, calendula, carnation, catnip, chamomile, cinnamon, clove, geranium, lavender, lemon, lemon balm, rose, thyme

COLORS: Pink (romantic love), red (passionate love)

RUNE SYMBOLS: Fehu, Kenaz, Gifu, Wunjo, Beorc, Ing

READING LIST

Here are some of the books I have found useful either in my own practice or as recommendations to others—or both! Hopefully they will help you as you continue your journey into the magical world of Witchcraft.

Goddesses

ALEXANDER, SKYE. *Your Goddess Year: A Week-By-Week Guide to Invoking the Divine Feminine.* New York: Simon & Schuster, 2019.

AUSET, PRIESTESS BRANDI. *The Goddess Guide: Exploring the Attributes and Correspondences of the Divine Feminine.* Woodbury, MN: Llewellyn, 2009.

BLAKE, DEBORAH. *Modern Witchcraft: Goddess Empowerment for the Kick-Ass Woman.* New York: St. Martin's Essentials, 2020.

ILLES, JUDIKA. *The Element Encyclopedia of Witchcraft: The Complete A–Z for the Entire Magical World.* London: HarperElement, 2005.

KANE, AURORA. *Goddess Magic: A Handbook of Spells, Charms, and Rituals Divine in Origin.* New York: Quarto, 2022.

MONAGHAN, PATRICIA. *Encyclopedia of Goddesses & Heroines.* Novato: New World Library, 2014.

OSBORNE, KATE. *The Goddess Resolution: Restoring Harmony and Emotional Wellbeing Through Spiritual Connection.* Woodbury, MN: Llewellyn, 2022.

Witchcraft Basics and General Practice

BALLARD, H. BYRON. *Seasons of a Magical Life: A Pagan Path of Living.* Newburyport, MA: Red Wheel/Weiser, 2021.

BLONDE, JENNIE. *Hearth & Home Witchcraft: Rituals and Recipes to Nourish Home and Spirit.* Newburyport, MA: Red Wheel/Weiser, 2022.

BLAKE, DEBORAH. *The Everyday Witch A to Z: An Amusing, Inspiring & Informative Guide to the Wonderful World of Witchcraft.* Woodbury, MN: Llewellyn, 2008.

—————. *A Year and a Day of Everyday Witchcraft: 366 Ways to Witchify Your Life.* Woodbury, MN: Llewellyn, 2017.

—————. *The Eclectic Witch's Book of Shadows: Witchy Wisdom at Your Fingertips.* Woodbury, MN: Llewellyn, 2021.

BUCKLAND, RAYMOND. *Buckland's Complete Book of Witchcraft.* St. Paul, MN: Llewellyn, 2002.

—————. *Wicca for Life: The Way of the Craft—from Birth to Summerland.* New York: Citadel Press, 2001.

CUNNINGHAM, SCOTT. *Wicca: A Guide for the Solitary Practitioner.* St. Paul, MN: Llewellyn, 1988.

Herbs

CUNNINGHAM, SCOTT. *The Complete Book of Incense, Oils & Brews.* St. Paul, MN: Llewellyn, 1989.

————. *Cunningham's Encyclopedia of Magical Herbs.* St. Paul, MN: Llewellyn, 1985.

————. *Cunningham's Encyclopedia of Wicca in the Kitchen.* St. Paul, MN: Llewellyn. 1990, 2016.

————. *Magical Herbalism.* St. Paul, MN: Llewellyn, 1982.

DUGAN, ELLEN. *Cottage Witchery: Natural Magick for Hearth and Home.* St. Paul, MN: Llewellyn. 2005.

————. *Garden Witchery: Magick from the Ground Up.* St. Paul, MN: Llewellyn. 2003.

Rituals & Spellcasting

BLAKE, DEBORAH. *Everyday Witch A to Z Spellbook: Wonderfully Witchy Blessings, Charms & Spells.* Woodbury, MN: Llewellyn, 2010.

WEST, KATE. *The Real Witches' Year: Spells, Rituals and Meditations for Every Day of the Year.* London: Thorsons, 2004.

Sabbats & Lunar Lore

COLE, JENNIFER. *Ceremonies of the Seasons: Exploring and Celebrating Nature's Eternal Cycle.* London: Duncan Baird Publishers. 2007.

MANKEY, JASON. *Witch's Wheel of the Year: Rituals for Circles, Solitaries & Covens.* Woodbury, MN: Llewellyn, 2019.

MORRISON, DOROTHY. *Everyday Moon Magic.* St. Paul, MN: Llewellyn, 2003.

Personal Practices

ARDINGER, BARBARA. *Pagan Every Day: Finding the Extraordinary in Our Ordinary Lives.* San Francisco: Red Wheel/Weiser. 2006.

BLAKE, DEBORAH. *The Goddess is in the Details: Wisdom for the Everyday Witch.* Woodbury, MN: Llewellyn, 2009.

—————. *Everyday Witchcraft: Making Time for Spirit in a Too-Busy World.* Woodbury, MN: Llewellyn, 2015.

—————. *The Eclectic Witch's Book of Shadows.* Woodbury, MN: Llewellyn, 2021.

DUMARS, DENISE. *Be Blessed: Daily Devotions for busy Wiccans and Pagans.* Franklin Lakes, NJ: New Page. 2006.

KAUFMAN, ANGELA. *Queen Up! Reclaim Your Crown When Life Knocks You Down: Unleash the Power of Your Inner Tarot Queen.* Newburyport, MA: RedWheel/Weiser, 2019.

MANKEY, JASON. *The Witch's Book of Shadows: The Craft, Lore & Magick of the Witch's Grimoire.* Woodbury, MN: Llewellyn, 2017.

MOURA, ANN. Green Witchcraft: Folk Magic, Fairy Lore & Herb Craft. St. Paul, MN: Llewellyn, 1996.

MUELLER, MICKIE. *The Witch's Mirror: The Craft, Lore & Magick of the Looking Glass.* Woodbury, MN: Llewellyn, 2016.

MADAME PAMITA. *Baba Yaga's Book of Witchcraft: Slavic Magic from the Witch of the Woods.* Woodbury, MN: Llewellyn, 2022.

SYLVAN, DIANNE. *The Circle Within: Creating a Wiccan Spiritual Tradition.* St. Paul, MN: Llewellyn. 2003.

Correspondences & Reference

GREER, JOHN MICHAEL. *The New Encyclopedia of the Occult*. St. Paul, MN: Llewellyn, 2003.

GRIMASSI, RAVEN. *Encyclopedia of Wicca and Witchcraft*. St. Paul, MN: Llewellyn, 2000.

HOLLAND, EILEEN. *Holland's Grimoire of Magickal Correspondences: A Ritual Handbook*. Franklin Lakes, NJ: New Page Books, 2006.

ILLES, JUDIKA. *The Element Encyclopedia of Witchcraft*. London: Harper Element, 2005.

ROSÉAN, LEXA. *The Encyclopedia of Magickal Ingredients: A Wiccan Guide to Spellcasting*. New York: Pocket Books, 2005.